Yorkshire Dales
A DOG WALKER'S GUIDE

AF272928

Rob Godfrey

COUNTRYSIDE BOOKS
NEWBURY BERKSHIRE

First published 2011
© Rob Godfrey 2011
Updated & Reprinted 2015, 2017, 2019, 2022, 2025

COUNTRYSIDE BOOKS
3 Catherine Road
Newbury, Berkshire

To view our complete range of books,
please visit us at
www.countrysidebooks.co.uk

ISBN 978 1 84674 242 2

Cover picture supplied by
Roger Evans

All materials used in the production of this book carry FSC certification.

Designed by Peter Davies, Nautilus Design

Typeset by KT Designs, St Helens
Printed by The Holywell Press, Oxford

Contents

Appendix

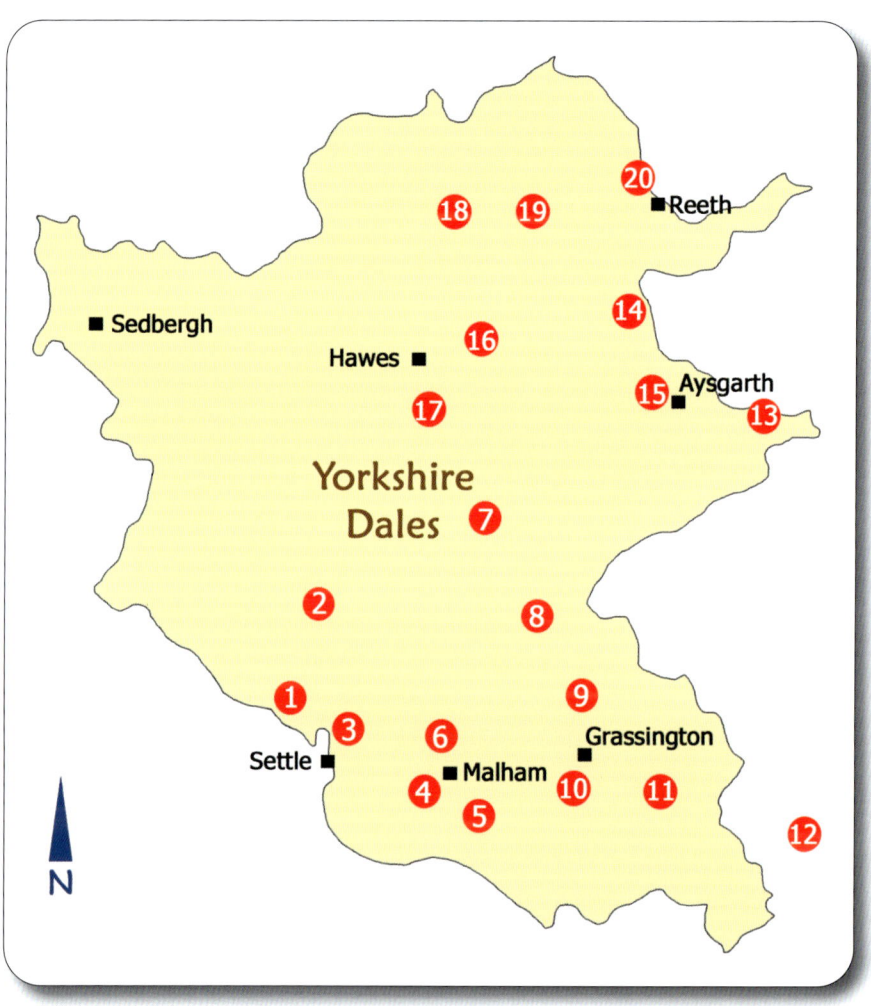

Area map showing location of the walks.

INTRODUCTION

I spent most of my childhood living close to the Derbyshire Peak District and developed a real love not just for walking but also for the landscape. When I moved to Leeds ten years ago the nearest good walking was now the Yorkshire Dales. For me a whole new landscape was waiting to be discovered, and I have not been disappointed.

The Yorkshire Dales includes the famous Three Peaks of Pen-y-ghent, Ingleborough and Whernside, as well as scores of lesser known, but equally dramatic crags and edges. You are never far from a waterfall either; some of them are impressive after rain and include (amongst many others) Aysgarth in Wensleydale, Linton and The Strid in Wharfedale, and Kidson in Swaledale. Other natural features include the famous cliffs and limestone pavements of Malhamdale, caves, pot-holes and many areas where wild flowers (including several rare species) still flourish.

If you have a dog, then walking can be great fun, seeing your best friend enjoying the open spaces, stretching their legs and enjoying all the sights and smells. All the walks in the book include areas where your dog can be let off the lead for a paddle, a run and a good sniff around in woods, fields or open moors (but see about moorland access below). However, if you know you can't rely on your dog to at least come back when called, it's better to err on the safe side and keep them on a lead most of the time, especially near livestock.

Most of the walks start from or near villages with pubs and cafés, so I have talked to the various landlords and owners to find out if they allow dogs in at least part of their premises. It does seem to be the case that if the pubs and tea rooms are dog-friendly, the local paths are as well. You can almost guarantee that if you keep coming across stiles that have been blocked by wire mesh fencing then the nearest pub won't allow dogs in either!

All of the pubs and cafés mentioned in the book allow dogs into some of their rooms. I would always telephone in advance to check for opening times and availability of food, though. A lot of the places mentioned have different opening and serving times in different seasons so again, check first if you are not taking your own food and drink on a walk.

The individual walk descriptions include references to suitable maps. The Harvey Yorkshire Dales Outdoor Atlas (1:40,000) covers the whole of the area and the Ordnance Survey covers the entire area at 1:25,000 scale with their OS Explorer Maps. The extra detail of field boundaries, etc on the 1:25,000 scale maps can be especially useful if you should ever find yourself 'temporarily disorientated' (we never mention the 'L' word).

Happy walking!

Rob Godfrey

ADVICE FOR DOG WALKERS

Livestock

The Yorkshire Dales is sheep country so expect to meet them almost anywhere on these routes, although it's rare that they will be grazing in all of the fields on a particular walk at the same time. You will also occasionally meet cattle in the lower lying fields and river meadows. I make sure Charlie, my Springer Spaniel, is always in sight and under control whenever there are animals nearby. In more restricted areas (indicated by various signs as you cross boundaries into them) this can mean having the dog on a short lead if he/she can't reliably walk to heel.

Large areas of the Dales are home to a number of ground-nesting bird species that are in need of protection (curlew, red grouse, skylark, lapwing and the oystercatcher). I am sure that roving bands of sheep disturb these nesting birds more than single dogs but nevertheless it is important that we don't add to the problem.

However, you are entitled to pass freely through any 'restricted' areas, *as long as you keep to public footpaths and bridleways*. Sometimes signs will state 'No Dogs' but these refer to dogs straying off the paths rather than the land being closed to all access. The Yorkshire Dales National Park Authority website has lots of useful information regarding the area in general but in particular about access. There is a very useful Q&A page on the topic in their Access and Recreation section: www.yorkshiredales.org.uk/.

Footwear, mud and ticks!

The only walk where you might get away with anything less than strong, waterproof walking boots or shoes is around Conistone Dib in the summer, but even on that relatively gentle walk there is a short section over very coarse limestone shingles. The rest of the walks all involve some rough tracks, crossing streams and often muddy ground, especially after any kind of wet weather (i.e. all year round!).

Not surprisingly with so many sheep around, I sometimes (though not often) find sheep ticks on Charlie, so it's worth having a check after a walk to make sure none of the nasty blighters have been picked up. Tick removers are available from pet stores to make it easy to get them off.

Drystone walls and stiles

In the Dales there are so many drystone walls, and stiles of various shapes and sizes through them, that I have only mentioned the ones that are difficult to negotiate because of their height or design. The worst culprits are the so-called 'ladder stiles'. Any of these with over three steps on either side can be

really difficult for dogs to climb over. It is often the case, too, that smaller dogs can negotiate these more easily than bigger ones. It should be possible to get round most of the walks in this book without having to carry your dog up and over stiles, as this can be a real pain if your dog is wet and/or muddy. Some of the walks are so appealing, however, that I have included them even if they have some of the dreaded ladder stiles where the average dog would need a hand to get over. Where possible I have described alternative routes if you want to avoid these stiles altogether.

Acknowledgements

Thanks to all at Countryside Books, to my partner, Janet, for all her support and encouragement throughout, and to Jill Handford for her help in testing the walks.

PUBLISHER'S NOTE

We hope that you obtain considerable enjoyment from this book; great care has been taken in its preparation. Although at the time of publication all routes followed public rights of way or permitted paths, diversion orders can be made and permissions withdrawn.

We cannot, of course, be held responsible for such diversion orders and any inaccuracies in the text which result from these or any other changes to the routes nor any damage which might result from walkers trespassing on private property. We are anxious though that all details covering the walks are kept up to date and would therefore welcome information from readers which would be relevant to future editions.

The simple sketch maps that accompany the walks in this book are based on notes made by the author whilst checking out the routes on the ground. They are designed to show you how to reach the start, to point out the main features of the overall circuit and they contain a progression of numbers that relate to the paragraphs of the text.

However, for the benefit of a proper map, we do recommend that you purchase the relevant Ordnance Survey sheet covering your walk. The Ordnance Survey maps are widely available, especially through booksellers and local newsagents.

Feizor, Wharfe & Town Head (Austwick)

Taking a dip in Austwick Beck.

This **relatively short walk** is full of charm from the word go. Feizor probably only just qualifies in size as a village but makes up for it in quality, with a picturesque ford at its centre. A small brook runs next to the road, adding to the charm of the many stone cottages, and the Pot Scar limestone crags provide an impressive backdrop. Feizor is at the end of a no through road just off the A65 so combines ease of access with a really tranquil atmosphere.

The hamlet of Wharfe nestles under some imposing rock formations that offer great views in return for a little effort climbing above the lane on our route round. After Wharfe you come to the Austwick Beck at a ford. Here a very picturesque stone bridge takes the footpath into Wash Dub Field, where in earlier times sheep would be washed in the dammed beck to remove parasites. Leaving the Beck you head over several large fields to Town Head just outside Austwick, before following a popular lane (and cycle path) back to Feizor, and now you can visit Elaine's Tea Rooms with a clear conscience!

There is plenty of scope for your dog to be off the lead along several of the tracks (but keep an eye out for cyclists). If your dog likes a paddle, there are a number of shallow streams for a dip (or a wash!).

Terrain
Just one short, but steep, ascent out of Feizor at the start of the walk.

Where to park
There is a small parking area in the centre of Feizor opposite the tearooms. **Sat nav:** LA2 8DF. **Maps:** OS Explorer OL2 Yorkshire Dales: South & West (but Feizor is just off the edge of this map), Harvey Superwalker Yorkshire Dales: Three Peaks, Harvey Outdoor Yorkshire Dales: Dales West (GR SD789677).

How to get there
Feizor is signposted off the A65 Skipton to Ingleton road, approximately 5 miles from the Settle roundabout and 7½ miles from Ingleton.

Nearest refreshments
Elaine's Tearooms, opposite the ford in Feizor, is open seven days a week all year round. This family-friendly tearoom has a car park and an outside seating area. They welcome dogs, provide water and treats, and even cooked sausages upon request. Payment is by cash only. ☎ 01729 824114.

Dog factors

Distance: 5¼ miles.
Road walking: 300 yards on the way out of Feizor on a very quiet (and gated) road, with another 300 yards on the road into Wharfe if you choose to avoid the ladder stiles. Later, approximately 200 yards through Town Head (Austwick).
Livestock: Watch out for sheep in any of the fields.
Stiles: This area does seem to have a lot of ladder stiles but most of them are quite small and the average dog can negotiate them with ease. Where there are larger stiles I have indicated alternative routes to avoid them.
Nearest vets: Dalehead Veterinary Group, Settle.

The Walk

. . . .

1 From the ford, walk up the lane with the tea rooms on your left, following the road round to the left as its starts to climb. Go through the gate and continue up the road as it climbs steeply away from the village. As the limestone rock formation rises ahead and the tarmac turns to rough gravel, look back for a fine view over the village.

Continue past the limestone rocks and when the lane levels out you will see **Pen-y-Ghent** in the distance to the north-east. Ignoring the signposted gate to the right, go through the gate crossing the track straight ahead and on to where a drystone wall runs in from the left. Shortly along this wall a rather steep ladder stile stands by a signpost indicating 'Wharfe ¾ mile'.

2 There is now a choice of routes either over a series of stiles across several fields, or continuing down the track, leading eventually to a short roadside walk. The walk over the fields is more scenic but the track and road are easier on your dog. If you choose to go over the stile, cross the field, heading downhill and skirting **Wharfe Wood** on your left. The easy-to-follow path crosses eight small fields and two streams before it meets the tarmac road just outside **Wharfe**. At the last stile into the lane turn left along the road (3).

If you want to avoid the ladder stiles, then continue on the main track, following it down past **Higher** and **Lower Bark House** until it meets the road, where you turn left towards **Wharfe**.

3 At a sharp left turn in the road follow the signposted bridleway to **Crummack** on the right. Follow the bridleway through and out of the hamlet of **Wharfe**, when it narrows to a tree-lined lane before heading up the dale.

4 Not far out of **Wharfe** a gate on the right indicates access to some open land. Here you can choose to go away from the bridleway and climb a little way up the hillside to gain some superb views over **Austwick** to the wide **Wenning valley** in the distance. Follow the path of the bridleway from above and drop back down to it as the **Austwick Beck** comes into view.

5 The bridleway leads down to **Austwick Beck** at a ford and the stone bridge that takes the footpath into **Wash Dub Field**. Cross the smaller stone slab bridge over the beck and follow the path at first left and then right towards a small gate in the drystone wall. Go through the gate into a larger field that dips then rises up in front of you. The path here is none too clear, but keep going up and bearing slightly left. Eventually as the shallow hill flattens out, a drystone wall will come in at right-angles from the left. There are stone steps over the wall leading into a second large field but now the green path is clearer to see and follow. As the ground slopes down you emerge through a shallow ridge of limestone. Continue through the field to cross a ditch fed by a spring. Bear slightly to the right this time. Eventually you approach a farm track running down to **Sowerthwaite Farm**. Cross the track and go through a gated stile opposite. The path ahead rises up to the next drystone wall. Go through the wall and then downhill (with the road now on your right) towards **Norber Sike** clearly visible in the valley bottom.

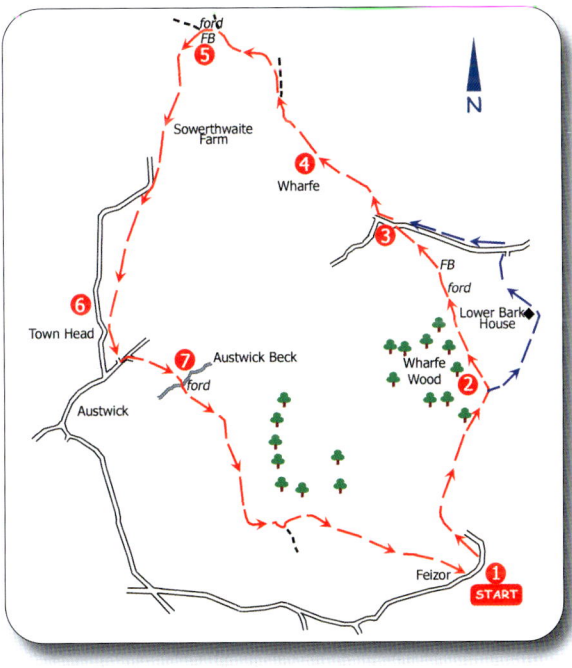

Cross the beck by the footbridge and walk on up to the gate by the stone building. Go through the gate and follow the wall to your left up to the corner of the next field. Go through the gated stiles on each side of **Thwaite Lane** to walk downhill with the drystone wall on your left. Follow this down to a stone stile that leads you into the back of **Town Head**.

6 Walk by the right side of the house and you will see a signpost pointing down and through a gate by a garage. Follow this down and out to the tarmac road on your right. Walk down the road to the T-junction and turn left. Walk about 100 yards down this lane and turn right down the lane signposted 'Pennine Bridleway Feizor 1¾ miles'. As the track reaches the end of the second field on your left an attractive stone footbridge (**Flascoe Bridge** on the OS map) takes you back over **Austwick Beck**.

7 The rest of the way back is easy to follow (at any junctions take the indicated bridleway direction to **Feizor**), just keep to the main track, but watch out for cyclists.

To Crummack Dale and Back

Below Moughton Scars.

This is a fine walk with some outstanding scenery, utilising a small section of the well-trodden Three Peaks Walk between Pen-y-Ghent and Ingleborough. There are just two ladder stiles to get over but it's worth it for the dramatic views and variety of the landscape. Once you have walked up and away from Horton there is a great feeling of space and freedom on top of the Sulber plateau. The large amphitheatre-like bowl at the head of Crummack Dale is equally impressive, followed by very peaceful walking in the dale itself along drystone walled lanes that feel like they have been there for hundreds of years. Climbing back up onto the Moughton limestone pavement gives rise to another great viewpoint before heading back down to Horton. The route also takes you through the Ingleborough Nature Reserve.

Terrain

A number of short but steep ascents/descents but nothing too taxing.

Where to park

There is a pay and display public car park with toilets in Horton-in-Ribblesdale. **Sat nav:** BD24 0HD. However, it is very popular with walkers so get there early on summer weekends and bank holidays. Limited parking on the road outside the car park and near the station. **Maps:** OS Explorer OL2 Yorkshire Dales: South & West, Harvey Superwalker Yorkshire Dales: Three Peaks, Harvey Outdoor Yorkshire Dales: Dales West (GR SD806725).

How to get there

Horton sits on the B6479 that runs through Ribblesdale, from Settle in the south, up to Ribblehead where it meets the B6255 that runs from Ingleton over to Hawes in Wensleydale. The car park is situated on the main road through the village centre. Horton-in-Ribblesdale station is on the Settle-Carlisle rail line and trains run approximately every two hours in each direction south to/from Settle and north to/from Carlisle (see www.settle-carlisle.co.uk for details).

Nearest refreshments

The Crown Hotel in Horton does not allow dogs in the bar due to space, but there is an outside seating area where dogs are welcome. See their website for opening times and the menu: www.crown-hotel.co.uk.

The Walk

. . . .

1 Starting facing the main car park in **Horton-in-Ribblesdale**, take the footpath to the right that leads onto the footbridge over the **River Ribble**. Where the footpath meets the main road, turn left and head up towards the railway station at the top of the hill. Go straight ahead into the station, following the footpath sign directing you to Crummack Dale (2 miles).

Dog factors

. . . .

Distance: 6½ miles.
Road walking: Some 200 yards on the B6479 between the main car park and the station (but not if you come by train), plus 300 yards down a quiet, single-track road at the end of Crummack Dale.
Livestock: Expect sheep almost anywhere on this walk.
Stiles: Just two ladder stiles that are unavoidable.
Nearest vets: Dalehead Veterinary Group, Settle.

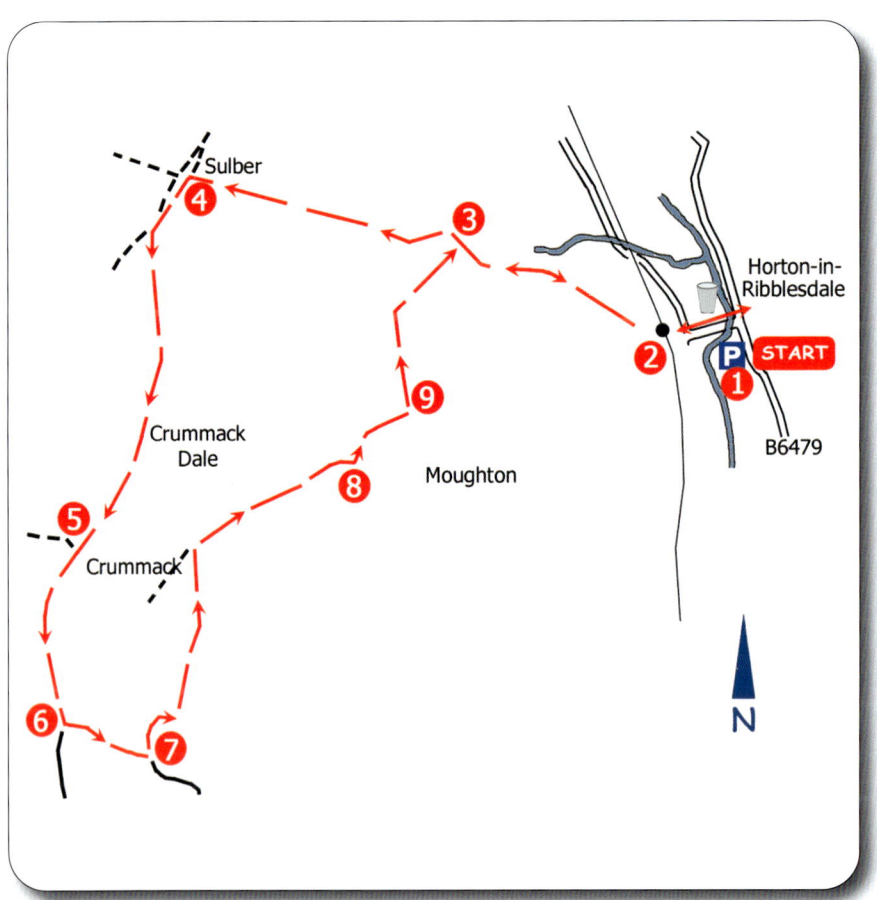

2 Cross the railway line (with care!) and go up the slope on the other side and into the field through the gate. There is now a clear path to follow, first through a gate in the opposite drystone wall and then turning right over the undulating field, crossing the farm track (to **Beecroft Hall farm**) and making for the wooden gate on the same path. Go through this gate and cross the field to another gate that marks the entrance into the **Ingleborough National Nature Reserve**. Here a notice-board gives you some information about the area. Follow the main path as it now starts to climb up the dale side. Turn left by the first cairn with a yellow-topped post. Continue upwards following the path, past another yellow-topped post until you reach a signpost (3) indicating Austwick 3½ miles (to the left) and Ingleborough 3 miles ahead. You will return to this point from the **Austwick** direction at the end of the walk.

❸ Continue ahead in the Ingleborough direction as the path leads you towards another gate in a drystone wall. Through the gate the path leads up and on to **Sulber Nick**, across the Sulber limestone plateau. It is advisable to keep your dog close by as there are lots of potentially hazardous holes on the plateau.

❹ As the path starts to rise again, there is a signpost indicating a bridleway to Clapham (3¾ miles). Turn left towards **Clapham** to follow the path until it eventually meets a gate ('**Sulber Gate**') and a ladder stile in a drystone wall. Luckily you can go through the gate and almost immediately turn left through a smaller gate. At this point a surprisingly dramatic view opens up as you look out over the head of **Crummack Dale**. The floor of the large amphitheatre-like depression is made up of a limestone pavement on which are the faint remains of an Iron Age settlement.

Follow the path down into the intriguingly-named **Thieves Moss**, where it seems to fade away as the soil thins and the limestone pavement begins. However, if you keep an eye out for boot marks and shorter grass you should be able to make out the path as it wends its way between the rock formations. Pretty soon the path becomes more distinct and heads off the pavement in the direction of the main valley. A drystone wall eventually appears and this has to be crossed via a ladder stile (this is the 'Beggar's Stile' shown on OS maps). At least now the path ahead is clear – a very pleasant green way across a large

A photo opportunity for Charlie near Wash Dub Field.

descending field. Take time to look back at the imposing **Moughton Scars** behind you.

You are now going gently downhill, following the path as it meanders across a large grassy area, always heading down the valley. After a while some trees come into view and a drystone wall runs in from the left. The path approaches and then hugs the wall as it leads you closer to the trees. Go through the gate (marked with yellow-topped poles) following the wall on your left, passing the signpost indicating that it is 3½ miles back to Horton.

5 Over the wall is a small copse, with **Crummack farm** behind. A couple more gates (with yellow signs on the posts) lead you on to the gravelled track running down the valley that you follow until a lane (signposted 'Wharfe 1¼ miles') runs in from the left.

6 Turn down the lane towards Wharfe, following it until it meets the **Austwick Beck** at a ford. This area is described in the previous walk.

7 Continue on the lane away from the ford and within 100 yards turn sharp left into a lane going back up the valley, bounded by drystone walls on either side for much of its length. When the drystone walls run out, the path/track continues to rise through the bracken-covered hillside, eventually leading onto the limestone paving of **Moughton**. At the top of the rise are convenient flat limestone rocks where you can sit and take a break, with long views down the valley you have just climbed out of.

8 With your back to the valley path turn left into the flat pavement area, initially looking out for small cairns to guide you first in a northerly, then easterly, direction, passing some disused stone grouse-shooting butts on the way. The path runs up to a drystone wall running north/south and here you have to go over the second (and last) ladder stile of the walk.

9 The signpost points in the return direction to **Horton** (1¾ miles away). Once over the stile turn left (north) to follow the path as it hugs the wall (to your left), following it up to and through the next incoming wall to the signpost to **Horton**, now only 1½ miles away. Follow the path as it heads back to the signpost at point 3 of the walk and heading right, retrace your steps back down to **Horton**.

3

Langcliffe & Winskill

Below Attermire Scar.

This is a gem of a walk, starting in a picturesque village and quickly taking you up amongst some very scenic limestone hills littered with interesting rock formations and high crags. In the warmer months this is an ideal walk on which to take along a picnic and take time out to sit and enjoy the many views. Langcliffe is an attractive little place and at weekends there is often something going on in the church or chapel near to the car park, usually involving tea and cakes. Trading started early around Langcliffe. Stone axes from Langdale, in the Lake District, have been found in the area, and in the Victoria Cave, above the village in Langcliffe Scar, were found a fragment of marble from Italy and coins that had been minted in the Roman provinces.

The limestone rocks in this area provide growing habitats for a wide range of plants that are rarely found elsewhere. The route passes through the edge of Winskill Stones Nature Reserve and if you look closely in the grass in spring and summer anywhere on this walk you will doubtless soon find a selection of wild flowers. It would be worth carrying a reference book and checking out your finds – but please don't pull them up (find out more about the reserve at www.plantlife.org.uk/nature_reserves/winskill_stones/).

As you are walking on limestone there is little or no surface water so it would be a good idea to take some water for your best friend on warm days. Your dog is going to enjoy the open spaces and most of the paths and tracks down from Winskill are safe enough (and sheep free) so you can take off the lead.

Terrain
Footpaths (some rough in places), green tracks, and paths through meadows. Short steep ascents/descents in a couple of places. As it is limestone country (and thus well drained) the walking is seldom muddy.

Where to park
There is a reasonably-sized free car park next to the church in Langcliffe that seldom fills up. **Sat nav:** BD24 9NN. Alternatively the roads in the village are quite wide and there are plenty of parking places without blocking off access for residents. **Maps:** OS Explorer OL2 Yorkshire Dales: South & West, Harvey Outdoor Yorkshire Dales: Dales South (GR SD823650).

How to get there
Travelling from the east or west along the A65 take the road into Settle (B6480 both directions). Continue through the centre of Settle and after passing under the railway arch on the way out again take the signposted road (B6479) to Langcliffe and Horton-in-Ribblesdale. Follow this for about ⅔ mile and turn right at the first sign for Langcliffe. Follow this (Main Road) through the village until you see the car park just opposite the church. Travelling south down Ribblesdale, turn left at the Langcliffe signpost and follow this road (New Street) until it runs into Main Street. Turn left here and continue up to the car park opposite the church.

Dog factors

Distance: 4½ miles.
Road walking: Limited to a short stretch getting out of Langcliffe and about 100 yards on a very quiet lane.
Livestock: Sheep graze in nearly all the fields.
Stiles: Plenty of these and all but one are easily negotiated. There is just one ladder stile over which your dog might require carrying.
Nearest vets: Dalehead Veterinary Group, Settle.

Nearest refreshments

There are no refreshment facilities in Langcliffe but plenty in nearby Settle. The Golden Lion on Duke Street is dog friendly and welcomes dogs inside. ☎ 01729 822203.

The Walk

① From the main car park in the village, cross the road and turn left and walk up the lane about 30 yards to the signpost to **Settle** on the right. Go through the gate and climb up to the top of the field, turning right after going through the gate at the top. Keep in this same (southerly) direction and eventually the path runs alongside a drystone wall with overhanging trees on your right. Ahead extensive views over **Settle** soon open up. Keep on the path up to and through a gate, heading in the same direction. Crossing the next field a ladder stile appears in the corner ahead but luckily there is also a gate to the left to get through the wall. The path now merges with a wider bridleway (from Settle to Winskill) heading downhill. This bridleway is often used by mountain bikers, so keep a look out for your best friend's safety. Going through the gate across the bridleway continue until a signpost on the left, showing 'Malham 5 miles', indicates it is time to start climbing again.

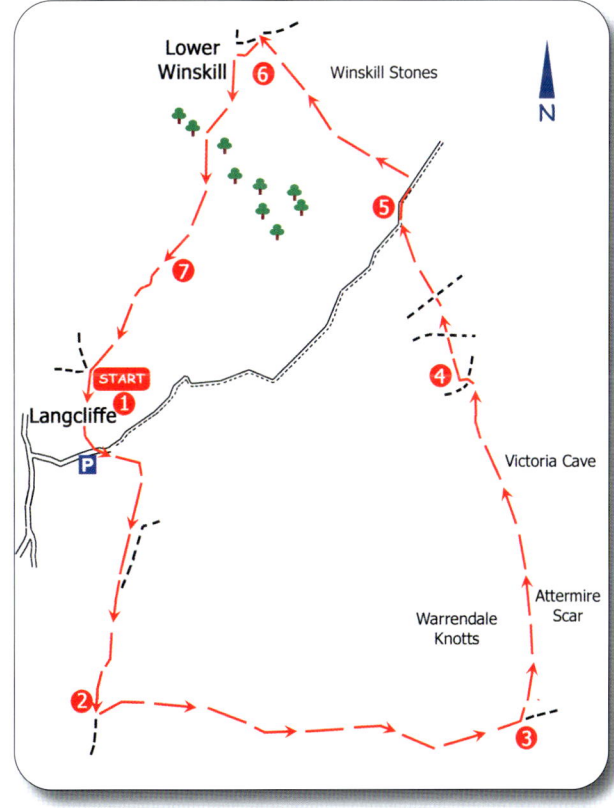

② Follow the path uphill and soon over a crumbled drystone wall. The path now curves upwards to become a wide green track. As you get higher you can see ahead (on a clear day) a trig point near **Warrendale Knotts**. At this point you can also see **Pen-y-Ghent** in the far distance over to your left. Keep climbing up to the drystone wall and turn right with the path (keeping the wall on your left). The broad green path takes you up to a damaged gate that at the time of writing was passable either by stepping over it or squeezing through the stile on the left. After the gate the path divides but either route leads you to the same place. The limestone rock formations of **Warrendale Knotts** on your left now get really interesting and more dramatic as you start to head gently downhill.

In the valley ahead there is a clear divide in the landscape where the limestone ends and over to the right the gritstone of the **Scosthrop Moors** begins. The much darker acid grassland and rough pasture dominating **Scosthrop Moors** stands in sharp contrast to the grey/white crags and bright green grass on the limestone.

The two paths soon merge again and run down to a drystone wall with a ladder stile. Luckily there is a hole in the wall about 70 yards off to the left to get your dog through if it's not happy with the (relatively low) stile. Walk ahead up to the signpost on the right and then bear left in the indicated direction of **Victoria Cave**, ½ mile.

3 The path now climbs left up the hill with the dramatic **Attermire Scar** ahead and right. Follow the path over boulder-strewn grass up to and through a gate

Limestone pavements on the way to Upper Winskill.

in the drystone wall, then turning left to continue upwards. The path soon levels off and now the rest of the walk involves little or no climbing so you will have lots of time to look around and enjoy the scenery. The wide green lane runs under the **Attermire Scar** to your right with equally interesting rock formations on your left. The path now heads to the right when a drystone wall crosses between the hillsides. Walk on through a number of gates as you skirt the foot of the crags. There are signs further along for the **Victoria Cave** with a mixed message telling you where it is but not to go too near it! The entrance is large and you can get an impressive view without actually going in (keep your best friend under control here). Continuing along the main route, a gate leads to a junction with a wide gravelled track. Turn sharp left and go through the gate heading downhill.

4 This track leads down to **Langcliffe** (offering an escape route if the weather turns). A little way down the track take the first 'green' path to the right, crossing the field and leading eventually to the first and only ladder stile that is not easy to get round. Take care getting yourself and your dog over this (at the time of writing part of the wall has crumbled away and my Springer could get up and over the stile quite easily). Once over, continue in the same direction on the broad green track as it now starts a gentle descent away from the limestone heights. Soon a metalled road comes into view and the path heads towards the cattle grid on the right.

5 Go round the cattle grid and continue on the roadside for 100 yards before turning left down the lane signposted for Stainforth, 1¾ miles. Opposite the lane is a small car park with an information board with details about the **Winskill Stones Nature Reserve** that covers the area above and behind the car park. It is worth a read and also maybe a detour to explore some of the area. Walking down the lane to the hamlet of **Upper Winskill** on a clear day you can see **Ingleborough**, one of the Three Peaks, on the horizon.

6 When you reach **Upper Winskill**, the signpost seems to point in more directions than there are paths! However, you want to turn left down the signposted direction to **Langcliffe**, going through a gate signed **Lower Winskill**. Continue down this lane until a signpost on the left indicates a footpath to Langcliffe. Go through the gated stile and cross the field, heading for the corner opposite where a gate and stile lead into a very pleasant footpath with fine views of **Langcliffe**, lower down the valley.

7 Keep heading down and the path levels out, leading eventually to a lane between drystone walls. Follow this lane all the way into **Langcliffe**; turning left at a crossroads with another lane will lead you into the back of the car park.

4

A Malhamdale Circuit

Looking down from Tranlands towards Malham.

Above **Malham is the famous cove,** a huge natural amphitheatre formed from the limestone. The river that once flowed over it is now a small stream that sinks into the limestone pavement below the Tarn, emerging at the foot of the cove and eventually becoming the River Aire. The dramatic location has been used for filming, including, recently, *Harry Potter and the Deathly Hallows, Part 1*. Nearby is the impressive gorge of Gordale Scar and, of course, the Pennine Way passes through here so it's a very popular place for walkers. The area was also the inspiration for Charles Kingsley's *The Water Babies*.

This walk leads you away from the bustle of Malham down the side of Malham Beck (that starts life flowing out from under the rocks at Malham Cove) to the 'official' start of the River Aire. Further round the route, Kirkby Malham is a small, very attractive village with the welcoming Victoria Inn to tempt you to a short detour. The 8th-century church of St Michael the Archangel is often called the 'Cathedral of the Dale'. As it is approximately halfway round the walk this might be a suitable place for a break. From Kirkby Malham you head out through some very pleasant lanes and fields before returning to Malham.

Dog factors

Distance: 3¼ miles.
Road walking: 200 yards on Cow Close Lane out of Kirkby Malham.
Livestock: You may encounter llamas near the beginning of the walk. They seemed quite shy and not at all aggressive when I walked through their field, but my experience of them is very limited so I did not get too close. There may also be sheep in the fields.
Stiles: Two ladder stiles fortunately having gates or holes in the wall next to them.
Nearest vets: Dalehead Veterinary Group, Settle.

Terrain
Some short but steep ascents/descents but nothing too taxing. Several streams on the way round too, suitable for a splash!

Where to park
There is a pay and display public car park with toilets in Malham **Sat nav:** BD23 4BY. However, it is very popular with walkers so get there early on summer weekends and bank holidays. There is very limited parking on the road in Kirkby Malham if you wanted to start the walk from there. **Maps:** OS Explorer OL2 Yorkshire Dales: South & West, Harvey Outdoor Yorkshire Dales: Dales South (GR SD899627).

How to get there
Malham sits at the head of Malhamdale and the main way in and out is via the minor road from Gargrave on the A65 if you are coming from the east (Skipton) or from the minor road from Coniston Cold if coming from the west (Settle).

Nearest refreshments
The Victoria Inn at Kirkby Malham is just a short detour off the route and welcomes dogs in the lounge. The Old Barn café in Malham welcomes walkers and their dogs inside. It also has an outside seating area. See their website for the menu and opening times: https://oldbarnmalham.co.uk/tea-room.

The Walk

❶ Leave the car park in **Malham** by the main entrance and turn left towards the village centre. Almost opposite you will see a signposted path to **Hanlith**

Bridge. Cross the road and go through the gate into the field and follow the direction alongside the wall with **Malham Beck** on the other side. Walk up to and through the gate at the end of the field. Walking through this second field leads to another gate, followed immediately by a footbridge over **Tranlands Beck**. Walk straight ahead and through a gate, continuing straight ahead towards a gated stile. The next field is sometimes home to grazing llamas, a fact that Charlie found very interesting and a little scary.

Continue on through the next gated stile (that also has a gate next to it) and follow the path that leads alongside the mill race leading to **Scalegill Mill** (now converted into separate apartments) with the **River Aire** invisible for most of this section on the other side.

Emerging on the other side of the mill, bear right up the grassy bank where the path leads to a gap stile in the drystone wall. Looking back just before you go through the stile, there is a fine view over the mill and the **River Aire** with the limestone rocks of **Gordale Scar** visible in the distance. Follow the path through the meadow and a gated stile on the other side. Through this the

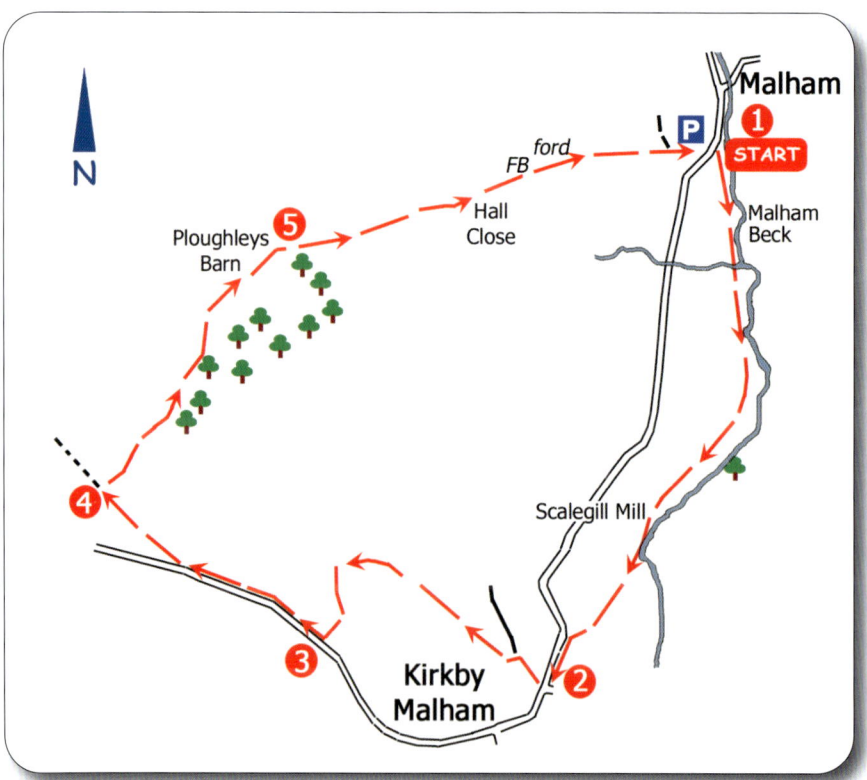

path leads down to the corner of a field against the road running out of **Kirkby Malham** towards **Malham**.

2 Go through the gated stile onto the lane and here you can choose to turn left and walk into the village, perhaps to visit the **Victoria Inn**, or cross the lane and go up the signposted footpath along **Cockthorns Lane**, continuing on our route.

Follow the track as it goes uphill until you get to a gap in the wall by a footpath sign to **Cow Close Lane**. Go through the stile and turn right to walk up the field, at first parallel to the lane. Keeping in the same direction, walk up to and past a single tall ash tree, with a house standing in the field behind. Go through the gate, walking forward about 70 yards before turning left to walk in front of the house. Ahead you should see a ladder stile over a wall that has convenient large drain holes if your dog is challenged by the ladder steps. Walk forward towards a gravelled track and turn left along it. Follow this through a gate and follow it as it curves right leading eventually onto **Cow Close Lane**.

3 Turn right here and walk up the lane for perhaps 200 yards before turning right along the track signposted 'Malham 1½ miles'. When the second field on the right is reached (just after the small copse on the left of the track) cross the ditch opposite an old leaning signpost for **Malham**.

4 Go over the wall or through the gate and down into the field beyond. At the bottom of this field is a drystone wall with some ruins behind it. Go through the stile and past the ruins to head down to a footbridge over a feeder stream of the **Tranlands Beck** that you crossed earlier. Up the other side to a fence and gate there is a signpost pointing across the field. Follow the direction of the signpost until a yellow-marked post indicates where the next gated stile sits. Head over this and cross the next field keeping the trees to your right. Another drystone wall is crossed via a ladder stile or the adjacent gate. The path now heads downhill towards a gate with a stone farm building (**Ploughleys Barn**) behind it. At this point the view ahead is of an extensive field system marked by drystone walls and **Gordale Scar** again in the distance.

5 Walk through this gate and bear right along a track leading to another stile and adjacent gate. Through the gate, Malham village is now visible amongst trees and in the near distance the roof of **Hall Close** is the direction to head for (not towards the first house behind the drystone wall ahead). Keeping the wall to your right, head down until the fenced end of the lane leading to **Hall Close** appears. Go through the gate (the stile to the left is not dog-friendly) and follow the lane past **Hall Close**, through the ford and all the way back to **Malham**.

Weets Top, Fairies & the River Aire

A quick plunge below Janet's Foss.

The Weets is a windy knoll a mile or so outside Malham. It sits at the top of a moor that gives you a real feeling of open space and some great views in all directions. Starting from the small village of Calton, this walk leads you up and over the moorland but then drops down into the very pleasant valley of the juvenile River Aire, using a section of the Pennine Way for the return journey, so it offers the best of both worlds.

The stretch over Calton Moor is a long, gentle climb eventually reaching 414 metres at Weets Top. Plenty of scope here for your dog to have a run around (as long as there are no sheep close by) and plenty of streams and bogs to splash around in too. It's worth stopping to look around here as on a clear day you can see for miles in most directions.

Dropping down from Weets Top the route runs close by Gordale Scar, an impressive gorge with a waterfall tumbling down it and well worth adding 20 minutes to your walk to have a look. The path takes you to the foot of the waterfall and from then it's a (often wet) clamber over rocks to get any further – this part is very steep and not suitable for dogs unless they are very agile. The stream below the gorge is made for dogs to paddle in.

Terrain
Some short but steep ascents/descents but nothing too taxing.

Where to park
There is limited parking on Kiln Hill between Airton and Calton, and around Calton. **Sat nav:** BD23 4AF. **Maps:** OS Explorer OL2 Yorkshire Dales: South & West, Harvey Outdoor Yorkshire Dales: Dales South (GR SD904592).

How to get there
Calton can be reached via Airton which sits astride the main road through Malhamdale. Take the minor road from Gargrave on the A65 if you are coming from the east (Skipton) or from the minor road from Coniston Cold if coming from the west (Settle).

Nearest refreshments
Due to its past strong Quaker influence (there is a Friends' meeting house in the village dating from around 1680) the village of Airton is sadly 'dry' except for tea, coffee and fruit drinks at the Town End Farm Shop & Tea Room. Dogs are welcome outside in the large patio area and there is a corner of the café inside where dogs are allowed. ☎ 01729 830902.

The Old Barn café in Malham welcomes walkers and their dogs inside. It also has an outside seating area. See their website for the menu and opening times: https://oldbarnmalham.co.uk/tea-room. The Lister Arms serves food and welcomes dogs in the bar area: www.listerarms.co.uk.

Dog factors
. . . .

Distance: 7½ miles.
Road walking: 300 yards down Hawthorns Lane from Weets Top and 100 yards in and out of Calton.
Livestock: There are often cows grazing on the track to Weets Top and in the fields by the Aire.
Stiles: Several ladder stiles but fortunately there are adjacent gates or holes in the wall next to them.
Nearest vets: Dalehead Veterinary Group, Settle.

The Walk

· ·

1 If you have parked by **Airton Bridge**, walk up **Kiln Hill** and into **Calton** (ignore the first right turn). Walk to the top of the village where **Calton Lane** meets **Kell Syke Lane**. By the left-hand kerb is a stone indicating **Manor Farm** with an adjacent signpost to our footpath (often covered by foliage overgrowing the wall). Take the gravelled track in the direction of the signpost leading to **Foss Gill**, then **Weets Top**. Continue down the track as it leads first to a ford (often dry in the summer) and then upwards, ignoring the left-hand fork. Soon the track runs up to a gate with a signpost to 'Weets Top 2½ miles'.

2 This track to **Weets Top** is popular with mountain bikers so keep a look out as they can approach quite silently. Go through the gate and follow the broad track through the large field with the gill on your right. There are often cows grazing here, so let go of your dog if the cows get too curious and they should leave you alone. The easy to follow track passes through two more gates (or you could take the ladder stiles if you and your dog are feeling energetic) before crossing into moorland, all the while with a drystone wall to your left. Ignore paths coming from left or right until you come to a signpost before a gate (**Weets Gate**) at the top of the moor. The route goes through the gate, but first look right towards the trig point marking **Weets Top** at 414 metres. There is a nice spot for a sandwich, with great views over the moors.

3 Go through the gate past the remains of an old wayside stone cross on the left and follow the track down and then left to the metalled **Hawthorns Lane**. With your dog now on a lead, turn left down this steeply descending lane, following it down to **Gordale Bridge** over **Gordale Beck** (where there is a refreshment van in summer).

4 A short distance before the bridge is a signpost indicating the footpath to **Gordale Scar** a detour worth making. Back on the main walk, cross over the bridge and take the signposted path on the left into the National Trust-owned **Janet's Foss** 30 yards down the road. Within 20 yards the path descends into a small wooded bowl into which drops the very attractive waterfall.

5 Jennet, the queen of the fairies, is said to live in a cave behind the falls or in another small cave to the right, so keep a good look out! This is a popular area in the summer for paddling and a picnic. The path continues down the wooded right-hand side of the beck. In spring the valley sides are cloaked in wild garlic. The clearly-marked path now follows the beck out of the woods

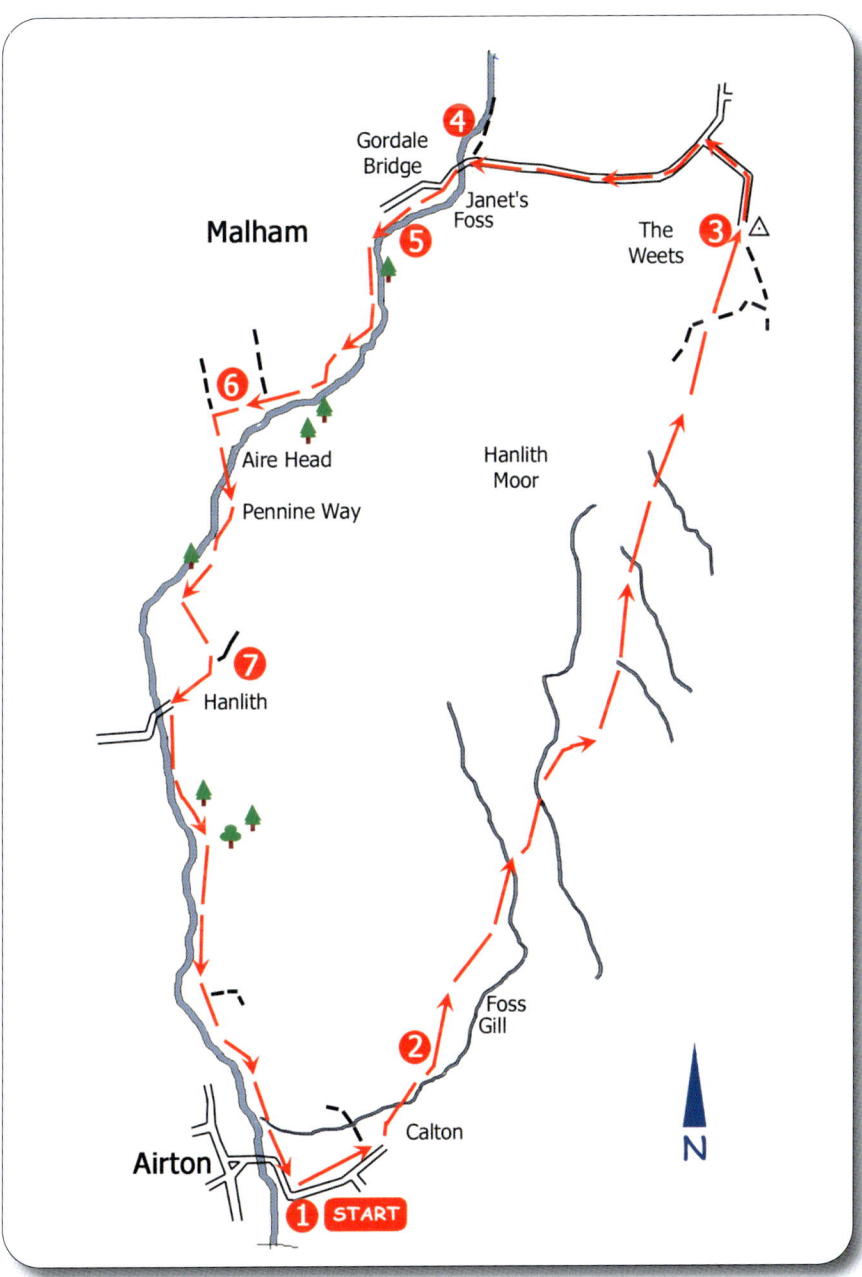

and across meadows through a number of gates leading away from **Gordale Beck**, until it reaches a T-junction with the **Pennine Way**.

6 Turn left down the signposted **Pennine Way** (in the indicated direction of 'Hanlith ¾ mile'). Walk along the valley bottom, going past **Aire Head** where **Malham Beck** and **Gordale Beck** meet to form the **River Aire**. After **Aire Head** the footpath starts to rise above the river, going through a number of gates as it leads you to the top of the hamlet of **Hanlith**.

7 The footpath drops you into **Windy Pike Lane** (better put the dog on the lead here) where you turn left down the road through **Hanlith**. As the road flattens out turn left just at the side of the bridge over the **Aire**, following the signposted **Pennine Way** to **Airton** (1⅓ miles). Go through the gate and now there is a pleasant path to follow the **Pennine Way** along the left bank of the **Aire** for most of the way back. After 100 yards look back and to your right you will see the impressive **Hanlith Hall**, first built in 1668. The **Pennine Way** leads us through many fields, but is always clearly marked. Where a significant path crosses our route, always take the signposted direction to **Airton Bridge**.

At the stone bridge at **Airton** our path meets the road from **Airton** up to **Calton**. Turn left and walk up the lane back to the start.

Charlie in a hurry to get going.

Four Limestone Scars from Malham Tarn via Langscar Gate

A wintry scene at Langscar Gate.

Here is a walk over some classic limestone features, with constantly changing views as it makes its way from Malham Tarn via Langscar Gate, passing under the limestone scars of Langcliffe, Attermire, Settle and Great Scar. There are a number of interesting diversions off the route that should not be missed, with some dramatic rock formations above Langcliffe to look out for, too.

Malham Tarn is the highest freshwater lake in England, created by glaciers thousands of years ago. On its western shore is Tarn Moss, a wetland haven for birds and wildlife. Malham Cove is a natural amphitheatre made up of

Dog factors

Distance: 9½ miles.
Road walking: 300 yards along Stockdale Lane, but it's a dead-end road leading only to a farm, so is never going to be busy.
Livestock: Grazing cows and sheep over most of the route.
Stiles: Gates or gated-stiles all the way with nothing that would tax the average dog or their handler.
Nearest Vets: Dalehead Veterinary Group, Settle.

curved limestone cliffs 80 metres high and 300 metres wide, formed after the last Ice Age. Above the cove and around Langcliffe are deeply fissured and fretted 'pavements' formed by chemical weathering due to acidic rain dissolving and widening the many joints of the limestone. The remaining lumps are known as 'clints' and the fissures 'grykes'. The grykes are home to many rare shade-loving plants – harts-tongue fern, wood-sorrel, wood-garlic, geranium, anemone, rue, and enchanter's nightshade. A number of areas along the route are designated as Sites of Special Scientific Interest (SSSI).

Of course you might not be able to take in all these in one trip, but that's a good enough reason to do this walk again another time. Dogs are going to love this walk too. There are lots of open spaces and tracks where it's safe to let them off the lead (as long as there are no sheep around, of course). It is pretty dry, with streams being few and far between (though there is a handy one by the car park) so it's advisable to take water for your dog.

Terrain

Some short but steep ascents/descents but nothing too taxing.

Where to park

Use the free car park by the Water Sinks just below Malham Tarn. **Sat nav:** BD24 9PT. **Maps:** OS Explorer OL2 Yorkshire Dales: South & West, Harvey Outdoor Yorkshire Dales: Dales South (GR SD894658).

How to get there

The car park can be reached from Malham by taking the Cove road past Malham Cove and turning right at the first crossroads junction. Alternatively take the Malham Rakes lane out of Malham and follow it up and round, turning left at the first junction and then on towards Water Sinks. Both routes involve steep climbs on narrow twisting roads that can be challenging if there is snow or ice about.

Nearest refreshments

In the summer there is an ice-cream van by the gate at the start of the walk. The Old Barn café in Malham welcomes walkers and their dogs inside. It also has an outside seating area. See their website for the menu and opening times: https://oldbarnmalham.co.uk/tea-room. The Lister Arms serves food and welcomes dogs in the bar area: www.listerarms.co.uk.

The Walk

. . . .

1 From the car park just below **Malham Tarn**, turn right to follow the road over **Malham Water** as it runs down from the tarn. Turn left to go through the gate where the signpost shows the way to **Malham Cove** and **Langscar Gate**. As you walk away from the road, the beck on your left starts to disappear into the ground (shown as **Water Sinks** on the OS map). The beck does not appear again until it emerges at **Airedale Head** below **Malham**. A little over 100 yards ahead another signpost points the bridleway to **Langscar Gate**. Follow the signed direction as the path goes up the hill. You are soon on a broad path that is joined a little further on by a path from the left (signed for Malham Cove). Keep straight on towards and through a gap in a drystone wall, after which the path bears left. After a small rise the track now heads down and you need to follow it as it bears right up towards the cattle grid on the Cove road that heads back down to **Malham**. Go by the side of the cattle grid and immediately turn right through a gate onto the public byway indicating 4 miles to **Cow Close** and **Langcliffe** – this byway leads through a number of gates all the way to the back of **Langcliffe**.

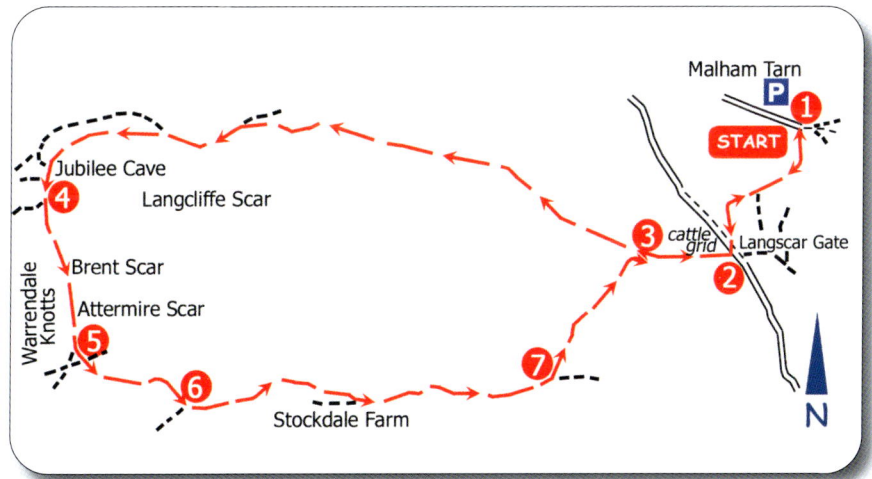

2 Follow the byway for ½ mile to where a signpost indicates a bridleway to **Stockdale Lane**.

3 The route will later return to this junction but for now continue ahead towards **Langcliffe** (rather disconcertingly the distance has grown by ¼ mile according to the signposts!). It's a very pleasant stroll now through a number of gates along a clearly marked track with no major ups or downs until you reach a gate after going past **Langcliffe Scar** on your left.

4 At this point the track now takes you between exposed limestone rocks and begins the drop down to **Langcliffe**. The rocks quickly rise up to your left to where the **Jubilee Cave** overlooks the track. A short distance further along, a signpost on your left shows where to turn off the track and head towards the **Victoria Cave**. Follow the path as it runs at the foot of the limestone scar (**Brent Scar**) close to a drystone wall on your right. After going through three small gates the path crosses a broad, open field and the intriguing shapes of the **Warrendale Knotts** rise up on your right. Soon the ground starts to descend past the **Attermire Scar** on your left. Ignore the gate and path off to your right but go down to the foot of the hill and, turning left, join the path to **Stockdale Lane**. From here it's a long, gentle climb back up to **Grizedales** about 3 miles ahead.

5 This section of the path can get waterlogged after rain as it takes you through the edge of the **Attermire Local Nature Reserve** and onto **Stockdale Lane**.

6 Turn left onto the tarmac lane and stay on this as it approaches **Stockdale farm** on your right in the valley. After the farm turning the road runs out into a track again. Follow this without a break until you arrive back at the signpost at point 3. As you climb up the road the round hump of **Rye Loaf Hill** (with **Kirkby Fell** behind) looms up on the right. In contrast to the green-covered limestone of the **Attermire Scars** and **Grizedales**, the acid soil here gives rise to a darker covering of heather and coarse grass. After the farm, count as you pass through three drystone walls.

7 Against the fourth wall, turn left at the junction to start the descent towards **Langscar Gate**. As the path descends, over in the distance (looking NNW) **Pen-y-Ghent** comes into view and then (NE) **Malham Tarn**. The route takes you past limestone pavements and through another three drystone walls before meeting the outgoing byway to **Langcliffe** again (3). Turn right and retrace your route back via **Langscar Gate**.

7

Buckden, Cray & Hubberholme

Heading up Buckden Rakes at the start of the walk.

Buckden lies on the Dales Way, at the northern end of the Wharfedale valley with the impressive Buckden Pike immediately to the east. The village was founded in Norman times and it lies on the route of the Roman road between the forts of Ilkley (*Olicana*) and Bainbridge (*Virosidum*). Our route takes us along Buckden Rake following the path of the Roman road, and up through Rakes Wood towards Cray before heading over Stake Moss.

Cray is a small hamlet and the last taste of civilisation before the road heads off over to Bishopdale. Our route then takes us up onto a very attractive plateau with extensive views down the Wharfedale valley beyond Kettlewell. These views down Wharfedale from above Hubberholme have been called spectacular and amongst the best in the Yorkshire Dales. You walk down from the plateau into Hubberholme, where Langstrothdale meets Wharfedale. This takes you past St Michael and All Angels, one of the oldest churches in Wharfedale. The farthest church up the dale, it was originally a Forest Chapel of the Norman hunting forest of Langstrothdale Chase, and dates from the 12th century. This church is the resting place of the ashes of the writer and playwright J.B. Priestley. You then head back to Buckden via a very pleasant walk along the banks of the River Wharfe, using the

Dales Way footpath, where there are many wildflowers in the spring and summer.

The navigation is easy with plenty of opportunities to let your dog off the lead (but always look out for sheep). Springs and streams are in plentiful supply so a water-loving dog is going to have a good time.

Terrain

Some short but steep ascents and a long steep descent down to Hubberholme.

Where to park

In the National Trust car park outside Buckden. **Sat nav:** BD23 5JA. **Maps:** OS Explorer OL30 Yorkshire Dales: North & East, Harvey Outdoor Yorkshire Dales: Dales South (GR SD942773).

How to get there

Buckden is on the main road through upper Wharfedale (the B6160) that runs from the B6265 at Grassington down to Skipton.

Nearest refreshments

The George Inn in Hubberholme has an outside seating area where dogs are welcome: www.thegeorge-inn.co.uk.

The Walk

. . . .

1 Starting at the National Trust car park, leave by the gate with the signpost to the public bridleway to **Buckden Pike** and **Cray High Bridge**. Follow the track known as **Buckden Rake** as it leads up the valley side and through two more gates. As you climb, fine views are revealed over **Hubberholme** and up towards **Yockenthwaite**. Keep to the main track, ignoring the right fork, going straight on up to another gate with a signpost on the other side of the drystone wall. Go through the gate and continue in the direction of **Cray High Bridge**.

Dog factors

. . . .

Distance: 4½ miles.
Road walking: Approximately 500 yards along a quiet lane between Hubberholme and Buckden.
Livestock: Look out for sheep along the paths.
Stiles: Just gates and no ladder stiles on this route.
Nearest vets: Kingsway Veterinary Group, Skipton.

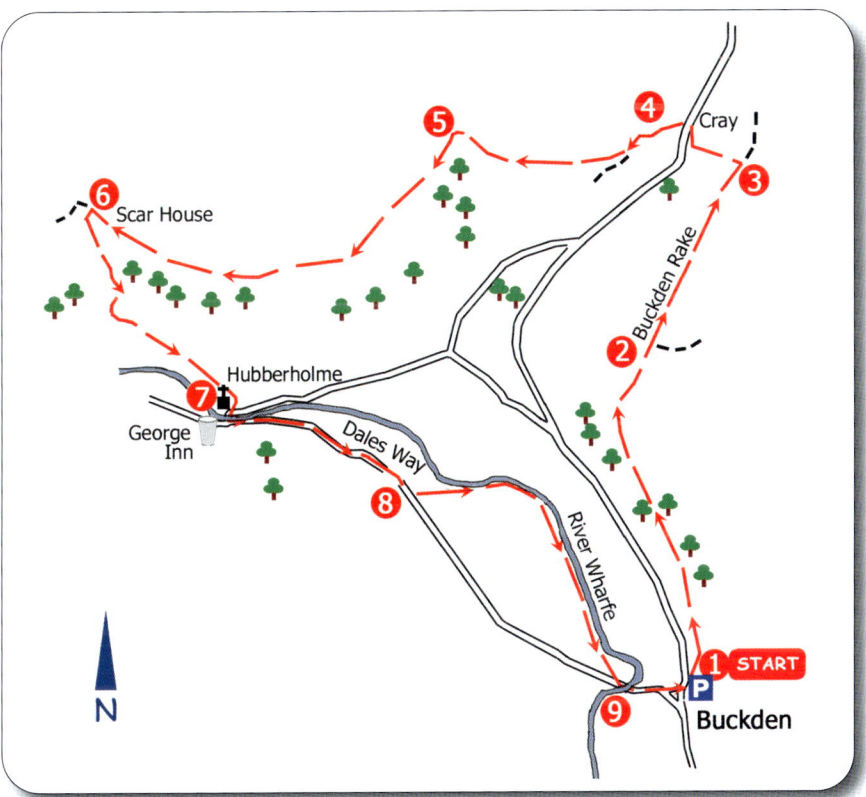

2 Follow the now green pathway towards another gate with an impressive large boulder as a gatepost. Looking ahead you can now see the road heading over to **Bishopdale** with **Buckden Pike** over to your right. Go through the gate and through three more fields. By the wall in the fourth field (the end of which is marked by trees) is a signpost directing you to the hamlet of **Cray** via a gateway in the wall.

3 Go through the gateway and straightaway you can see **Cray** on the opposite side of the road. Head down the hill towards the drystone wall on your right. Where it turns sharp right a signpost indicates the direction to follow. You finally end up against some stepping stones across the **Cray Gill** as it tumbles down the hillside.

4 Crossing the road, you will see the footpath sign to **Yockenthwaite** and **Stubbing Bridge**. Follow the track behind the White Lion (now closed) and take the path up to the right soon after. Continue up and round the farm buildings, through a gate and then a shallow ford. There is no further climbing on the walk and it is time to start enjoying the views and really relax. Follow the track in the same direction past a signpost that shows the footpath down to **Stubbing Bridge** (which can be ignored) and on past a second showing **Scar House** and **Yockenthwaite**. Head on over the field towards a building showing to the right of a drystone wall. Walk up towards the building and go through the gate, heading towards the right to follow the wall down towards the small valley ahead. Turn right round the end of the wall and you will see a footbridge to get you over the **Crook Gill stream** as it tumbles down from the high pastures.

5 Crossing over the footbridge, follow the path left as it now follows the edge of a broad shelf on a contour. Soon you will have extensive views over to **Buckden Pike** on your left and down the **Wharfedale valley** past **Buckden** and **Starbotton**, almost down to **Kettlewell**. There are several springs that emerge to your right and after rain some attractive small waterfalls make a pleasant backdrop for a sandwich stop.

Continue along the shelf up to and through a narrow wooden gate. A short distance further on you will see the farm buildings at the back of **Scar House** down to your left with a track going down and round it. At the time of writing there is a signpost indicating the path down to **Hubberholme** but it was, sadly, lying on the ground pointing skywards.

6 Ignoring the sign, drop down to this track and follow it through to the front of the house. Now you can see why the house was built here. There are fine views down the steep hill that leads us via the concrete track all the way down to **Hubberholme**. As you approach the village ignore the signpost at the back of the church, continuing through the gate and round the back of the church to emerge on **Stubbing Lane**. It is worth a visit to the church as it has a fascinating history and some interesting features.

7 Turn right and then go over the bridge, turning left to pass in front of the **George Inn**. Continue down the road until you come to a footpath sign indicating 'Buckden Bridge ¾ mile'.

8 Go into the field through the gate and now it's a simple matter to follow the well-marked path (recently re-surfaced) down to and alongside the **River Wharfe**. This stretch of the river has many wild flowers growing along the bank.

9 The path leads back to the road via a gate just before the bridge takes you over the **Wharfe** and back into **Buckden**. At the junction turn left to head back to the car park.

8

Kettlewell & Starbotton

Dwarfed by the landscape on Cam Head.

This is a really good walk, with great views up and down Wharfedale along the way. The route is easy to follow with plenty of signs and no tricky stiles to negotiate. Kettlewell is another attractive dales village with several tea rooms and pubs offering a range of refreshments. An annual Scarecrow festival is held here which is well worth a visit in its own right. Scarecrows first came to Kettlewell in 1994 when a fundraising event was organised for the local school that serves much of Upper Wharfedale with its villages, isolated hamlets and remote farms. The enthusiastic response of parents and residents led to over 100 scarecrows appearing in gardens, open spaces, hidden corners and even on rooftops. The event was successfully repeated and, growing year by year, now attracts thousands of visitors over a nine-day period in August.

There are a few springs around the route but it might be worth carrying additional water on a hot day so your dog can have a drink. As always there are plenty of sheep about, but also wide tracks where your dog can be off the lead.

Yorkshire Dales – A Dog Walker's Guide

Dog factors

Distance: 6¼ miles.
Road walking: Approximately 400 yards at the end of the walk through the minor village roads back to the car park.
Livestock: There may be sheep in almost any of the fields.
Stiles: None, just gates.
Nearest vet: Kingsway Veterinary Group, Skipton.

Terrain

Rough going on several of the tracks and two steep climbs.

Where to park

There is a car park near the bridge over the River Wharfe at the southern end of Kettlewell. **Sat nav:** BD23 5QZ. **Maps:** OS Explorer OL30 Yorkshire Dales: North & East, Harvey Outdoor Yorkshire Dales: Dales South (GR SD967723).

How to get there

Kettlewell sits on the B6160 that runs the length of Wharfedale between the A65 (Skipton to Kirkby Lonsdale) and the A684 through Wensleydale.

Nearest refreshments

The friendly Blue Bell Inn in Kettlewell welcomes dogs inside and has children's menus. There is a large outside seating area in front of the pub. Dogs are also welcome in their six bed and breakfast rooms:
☎ 01756 760230.

The Walk

1. Starting from the National Park car park, turn right to leave the village over the main bridge across the **River Wharfe**. Immediately over the bridge turn right onto a track that divides into two. Take the left fork to go up and through a gate just after the signpost indicating a bridleway to **Moor End** (our initial destination) and footpath to **Arncliffe**. Carry on along the main track, ignoring the footpath that leads to **Arncliffe** on your left. There are several gates to go through along this track that keeps to the drystone wall on your right. When the track splits into two, follow to the left up to another gate.

2. Take time to look back over **Kettlewell** (and catch your breath too) as you

continue up the steep valley side. When the track finally levels out you have the pleasure of extensive views up and down the dale with **Starbotton** (our second destination) coming into view further up the valley.

❸ The track now runs up to **Moor End farm** where you go through a gate into the yard. Turn left in front of the farmhouse and then right, walking round to the back where a signpost shows the direction to follow. The route now runs along a drystone wall up to another gate. Through the gate bear right (signposted again) and walk down to another signpost and gate. Go through the gate, bearing left now towards a signpost in the middle of the field. Follow the directed path towards a gate and go through the field directly ahead to yet another gate with a signpost behind it. Bear right and head down to a final gate, bearing left to start heading downhill quite quickly now.

❹ The path ahead is clear but the hillside drops away steeply to the right, so keep your friend close by. Soon the path runs up to a gate, letting you into a wood as it makes its way steeply downhill through a number of gates before the ground levels out in the valley bottom. The ground on either side of the path is boggy all year round so I would keep your dog to the path at least until you get to the footbridge going over the **Wharfe**. Now is an opportunity for a paddle as the river is shallow here (but watch out if it's in flood). The signpost also indicates a footpath heading back to **Kettlewell** along the **River**

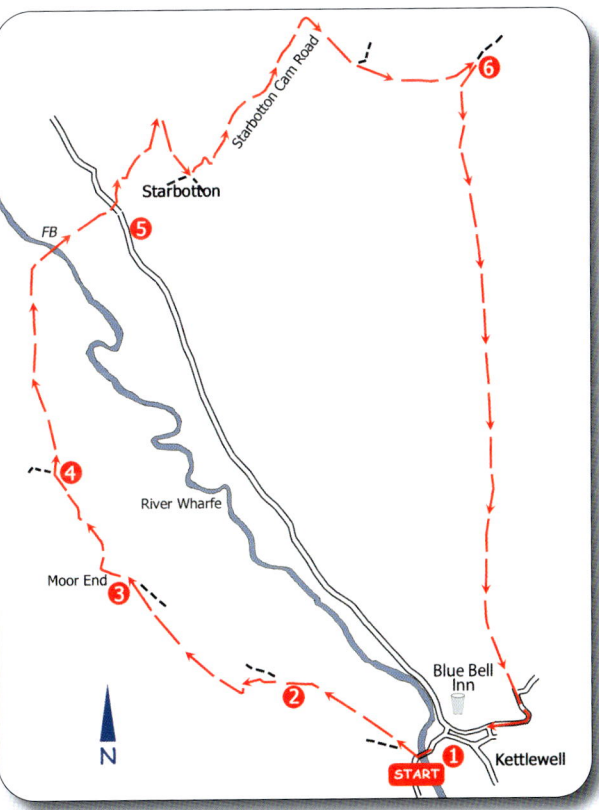

Wharfe. You might want to take this for a leisurely stroll back if you are not feeling too energetic. Otherwise, cross over the footbridge and go up the narrow lane that runs up to the main road through the valley.

At the top of Wibbertons Fields above Starbotton.

5 To the left is the village of **Starbotton**. Cross the road and turn left up the lane into the back of the village. Almost immediately on the right is a signed footpath back to **Kettlewell** (2 miles) – our route does not go this way, but it is an alternative, pleasant walk back through fields and keeps to the lower valley side.

Following the lane round to the right, keep walking until a signpost on your right indicates a public bridleway to **Kettlewell** (3½ miles). This is the **Starbotton Cam** road. Follow this track as it now climbs steeply out of the village and up onto the moor. As you climb, don't forget to stop and look up and down the valley for a different set of views. The main track continues to climb with three gates to go through. Ignore the track heading left just before the third gate.

6 As you go through the third gate the track now levels out and the bulk of **Great Whernside** comes into view ahead. As the track runs down to a junction, turn right towards **Kettlewell** (as shown on the signpost). The way ahead now is clear and straightforward as the track leads directly back down into **Kettlewell**. There are great views all round and you can enjoy this section knowing it is downhill all the way. When the track runs into a tarmac road, follow it down into the village.

9

Conistone Dib

Looking up the Dib away from Conistone.

This walk has become my local favourite over the years as it's a nice lengthy stroll, with some impressive open spaces and views. The varied scenery is based on the Yordale limestone terraces above the River Wharfe between Grassington and Conistone, giving rise to some interesting rock formations and limestone pavements. If you look closely, you will also find plenty of wild flowers, especially in the longer grasses.

A knoll with a very distinctive shape to the north-east of Conistone village, known as Conistone Pie, is visible from the main road down the valley (it really does look like a big pie). Look out too for the dry gorge above Dib Beck. This steep-sided dry valley has almost vertical sides to the east, with ash trees growing precariously out of crevices in the limestone on both sides. The route passes old field lime kilns where limestone was burnt to make agricultural lime, spread on the land to increase the productivity of the meadows and pastures. At the end of the walk a steep, narrow, rocky valley just outside Conistone shows evidence of an ancient, collapsed cave system that is a delight, with huge overhanging limestone walls.

For dogs there will normally be plenty of opportunities to be off the lead. On a hot day you might want to bring along some water though, as there are no springs or streams the whole way round.

Yorkshire Dales – A Dog Walker's Guide

Terrain

Very short steep ascents/descents in a couple of places (less than 50 yards anywhere). As it is limestone country (and thus well-drained) the walking is seldom muddy.

Where to park

If you park considerately you can leave your car on the roadside in Conistone village where the roads are wide enough. **Sat nav:** BD23 5HS. However, it is popular with tourists (and visitors to the Trekking Centre) so get there early on summer weekends and bank holidays. **Maps:** OS Explorer OL2 Yorkshire Dales: South & West, Harvey Outdoor Yorkshire Dales – Dales South (GR SD981674).

How to get there

Travelling north from Skipton on the B6265 and B6160, turn right at the first Conistone signpost 2 miles after Grassington. Travelling south down Wharfedale take the Conistone signpost about 200 yards past Kilnsey.

Nearest refreshments

Conistone is a very pleasant village that would be idyllic if only it had a pub of its own! Luckily there are some very good dog-friendly places not too far away in Grassington; the Devonshire Hotel in Main Street welcomes dogs in the bar area but not in the restaurant. See their website for the menu and opening times: www.thedevonshiregrassington.co.uk. The Old Hall Inn in Threshfield (www.oldhallinnandcottages.co.uk) welcomes dogs inside but again not in the restaurant area. Both these places serve food in the bar area.

Dog factors

Distance: 3 miles.
Road walking: 200 yards on quiet lanes within Conistone.
Livestock: It is rare for sheep to be in all the fields along the route. There are occasionally grazing cattle along the Dales Way.
Stiles: Plenty of these but all are gated. The one and only ladder stile sits over a crumbled drystone wall by a broken gate so it is easy to get round.
Nearest vets: Kingsway Veterinary Group, Skipton.

The Walk

❶ At the centre of **Conistone** is a small triangular green. Start by walking towards **Grassington**, away from the green, down **Grass Wood Lane**. After approximately 150 yards there is a signed footpath on the left, indicating 'Grassington 2½ miles', immediately before a cottage. Take this as it rises round the side of the cottage leading to a gate. If the gate is closed, there are almost certainly sheep in the field. If the gate is open, you are in luck and the large field will be empty and your dog can stretch his legs.

    The broad path/track rises gently as it hugs the drystone wall to your right. Follow this path up to and through another gate and across a wide field with expanding views over the **River Wharfe** to your right as the path climbs gently up. Looking up to your left you start to see the development of limestone outcrops that become more interesting as the walk develops. Look out for wild flowers too for the next mile or so as you walk over the grassy fields; there are also interesting fungi to be found alongside the path. Keep following the wide track as it makes its way up to another gate. Go through this and across another field that is home to large stands of bracken. A final gate leads you closer to a wide wooded gorge that comes into view on your right. As you drop down to the gorge the path turns left to run alongside the steeply dropping valley side. Watch your step here as the narrow path starts to climb up again. Now is a good time to find a flat limestone rock and sit and admire the view.

❷ The gorge is dry at the top, but out of sight below are a series of springs that feed into **Dib Beck**. The path now runs alongside a drystone wall for about 100 yards before going through a gated stile on the right. Through the stile

Approaching the dry gorge of Dib Beck.

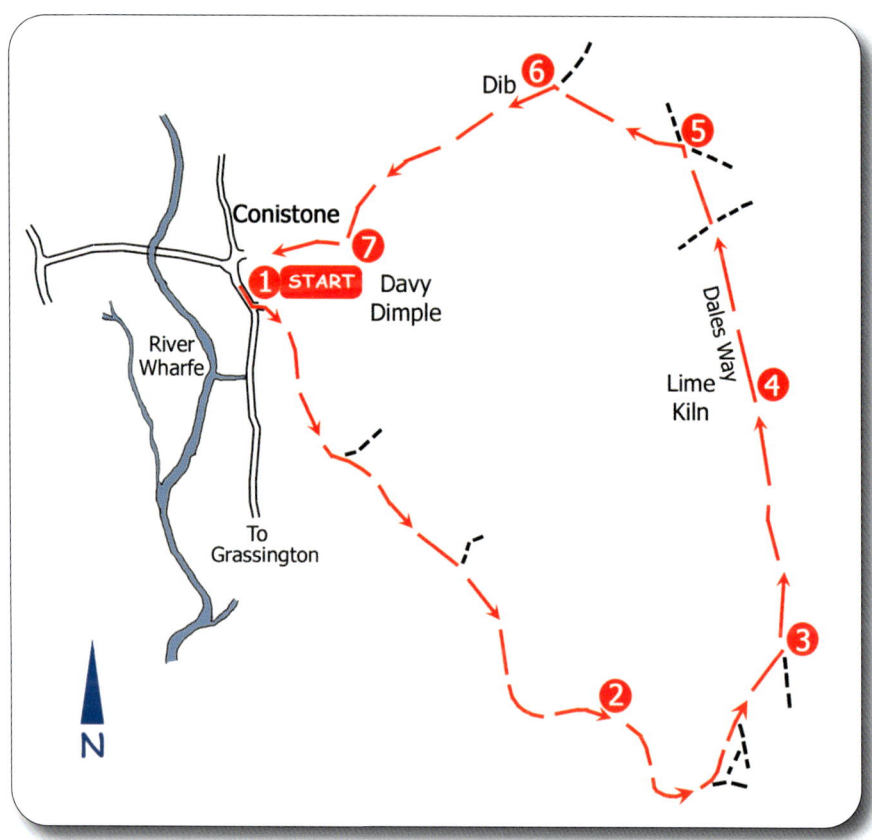

the path first drops down and then quickly climbs up a short rocky slope and through another (crumbling) drystone wall. You have just finished the most strenuous part of the walk! Follow the path as it gently rises past some gnarled and fallen hawthorn bushes towards **Bastow Wood**. Soon the drystone wall to your left has a ladder stile that you need to get over. Luckily there is a gate next to it and between that and the tumbled wall there is usually an easy way through for your dog.

On the other side of the stile the path leads off to the right into a broad open grassy plain. The green, well-cropped (by rabbits) paths are clearly visible for most of the year but in winter they can be almost invisible under just a few inches of snow. Follow the path away from the stile and the gate, ignoring the fainter path that crosses yours almost immediately and heads off to the right (in the wrong direction) towards **Grassington**. Looking forward you will see the path starts to gently descend as the mound to your left falls away. Another 150 yards on, veer left at a junction of paths and continue gently down. Away to the left are some very interesting limestone features. The whole of this area was the site of an Iron Age settlement and has many cairns and other features. Keeping in the same general direction the path eventually runs up to a gated stile. Just before this stile, the **Dales Way** from Grassington joins from the right.

❸ Go through the wall and look around as you are now in the middle of a large shallow bowl surrounded on all sides by limestone terraces, with drystone walls running along the horizon and not a sign of human habitation. Rabbits abound here and your best friend might be tempted to run after them. Do be aware that some of the exposed limestone is formed into the classic limestone pavement with many gaps between that might hurt the unwary (or excited) animal.

The path bears left across the next field towards another gate, passing some exposed limestone paving to your left on the way. Through the gate into the next field there is just the one path to follow. The path is now a delightful green lane that looks like someone has run along it with a lawn mower (but I think it's rabbits really) and begins to rise gently, eventually running between higher ground on both sides. At this point there are convenient limestone rocks to sit on and have a sandwich and a hot drink, whilst admiring the scenery.

❹ Carrying on gently upwards, there is an old lime kiln on your left just before you reach the brow of the rising land. From here it is all flat or downhill and as you progress great views of the upper Wharfedale valley open up in front of you. Eventually the spectacular **Kilnsey Crag** is visible, dwarfing the village below it. Keep on the main path through another two gated stiles. In this field there are occasionally grazing cattle. It's a big field and there is plenty of space to walk round any cows that happen to be dozing in the path. Through the last gated stile the path forks.

❺ Take the left-hand fork heading gently down in the signed direction to **Conistone**. The **Dales Way** continues on the right. Follow the left-hand path past a dew pond (a good place for a doggy swim when it is full) and into a narrow valley. At a gate at the bottom turn left into the main **Dib** (dry) valley again in the signed direction to **Conistone**.

❻ The valley is steep-sided and eventually narrows into a tight crevice less than a yard wide in places. This was evidently once a cave whose roof collapsed long ago. The path is now made up of coarse limestone rocks between a narrow defile with ash trees growing precariously out of the steep sides. As the valley begins to broaden out again, sadly you come to the end of the walk as you enter **Conistone** through a final gate. Walking down the lane, you come quickly back to the green.

10

Linton Moors & Meadows

The path to Tarn Lane.

This walk combines pleasant bridleways, tranquil hay meadows and windswept open moors. Once you have climbed up to Linton and Boss moors there are views all round and there is a great feeling of open space with not a single building or road in sight and just the cry of moorland birds for company (and the occasional bleating of sheep). On lower ground the hay meadows are a treat in early summer, awash with wild flowers. The bridleways and tracks bounded by trees and drystone walls are often lined with wild flowers and plenty of sloe berries to pick in the autumn (for your gin of course).

Some of the broad tracks are a safe place for your dog to be off the lead, but keep an eye out for occasional farm traffic. The smaller fields, enclosed by drystone walls will provide relatively safe off-lead areas too (assuming there is no livestock in them, of course). There are no difficult stiles to overcome and as long as you keep close control of your dog over the grouse moors it is dog-friendly all the way. There are several streams and springs for the water-loving dog to go for a paddle too.

Terrain

There are no steep ascents/descents over the whole route. Keep to the footpath through the old mine workings on Boss Moor.

Where to park

If you park considerately, you can leave your car on the roadside almost anywhere in Linton village. **Sat nav:** BD23 5HJ. However, it is very popular with tourists so get there early on summer weekends and bank holidays. **Maps:** OS Explorer OL2 Yorkshire Dales: South & West, Harvey Outdoor Yorkshire Dales: Dales South (GR SD996627).

How to get there

Travelling north from Skipton on the B6265, turn right at the first Linton signpost just after passing Swinden Quarry. This is Lauradale Lane and Linton is perhaps ½ mile away. Travelling south down Wharfedale take the Grassington signpost just opposite the garage at Threshfield. Turn almost immediately right (signpost to 'Burnsal B6160') and follow this road down under the old railway bridge before taking the next right into Linton village.

Nearest refreshments

The Fountaine Inn in Linton has seats outside looking onto the green and dogs are allowed inside too (wherever there are stone tiles on the floor), ☎ 01756 752210.

Dog factors
· ·

Distance: 7 miles.
Road walking: 200 yards on the B6265. Watch out for cyclists as the bridleways around Boss and Threshfield moors are popular mountain bike trails.
Livestock: Keep your dog under control over Linton Moor, where you will encounter not only sheep but also grouse and other wildlife.
Stiles: Plenty but all are gated or have an adjacent gate.
Nearest vets: Kingsway Veterinary Group, Skipton.

The Walk

1 Starting from the main bridge over the **Linton Beck**, with the **Fountaine Inn** to the left, leave the village along **Lauradale Lane** (B6265) towards **Cracoe**. Approximately 200 yards past the last house on the left you will see a bridleway signpost to **Tarns Lane** on the right. Walk up this gravel track lined with sloe bushes and many wild flowers in the spring/summer. The track rises gently, taking you over the old Skipton to Grassington railway line. If you look behind from here (in an easterly direction) you will see **Elbolton Hill** near **Thorpe**, which has long been called 'Hill of the Fairies'. As the track runs out at a tight left-hand bend there is a gate straight ahead leading into a grass-covered lane running gently downhill to the main Skipton to Grassington road, the B6265 (**Tarns Lane**).

2 There is no gate onto the road so make sure your dog is under control here. Cross with care and go straight onto another bridleway to **Cracoe**. Follow this roughly gravelled track as it gently climbs and makes its way along the back of **Swinden Quarry**. At some sheep pens on your left you will meet a gate signing the beginning of **Linton Moor**. For most of the following moorland (to waypoint 6 on the route) you are asked to keep your dog under close control as it is home to grouse and other birds as well as being grazed by sheep almost the whole year round. You are still free to walk with your dog as long as you keep to the bridleways and footpaths ('No Dogs' signs only refer to moorland off the path). Go through the gate and follow the track up the hill with **Eller Beck** running downhill on your left. Make for the stand of trees appearing directly ahead. As you close in on the trees you will see they occupy the opposite bank of the gully formed by **Eller Beck**.

3 Don't follow the main path here (as it drops down to ford the beck) but take the fainter path to the right, away from the beck. This path is not too distinct in its early stages but as it gently rises you will see **Hammerton Hill** ahead of you. After rain, parts of this path can be very soggy. Nearing **Hammerton Hill** the path crosses a small footbridge made of railway sleepers with **Tewit Mire** on your right (not shown on the Harvey map) – as the name suggests, it's a wet area! Follow the footpath now heading to the right of **Hammerton Hill** up the lower slopes of the adjacent **Blackstone Edge** leading to a gate. Go through the gate or over the ladder stile and forwards for 50 yards before coming to a T-junction. (If you take the right-hand path it will take you directly back along **Blackstone Edge**, eventually running into **Moor Lane** and **Threshfield**, a good escape route if the weather closes in.)

Take the left-hand path up the hill with **Hammerton Hill** now on your left. At the gate at the top follow the curving track as it makes its way over **Boss**

Moor. You are advised that much of the moor has old mine workings and it is safer for you and your dog to keep to the footpaths and tracks. Shortly the footpath meets another T-junction, turn right here to continue to a gate and through this over the moor. This track runs out at another T-junction where a footpath comes from the small car parking area on the left.

4 This car park is on **Boss Moor Lane** that runs up from **Hetton**. Looking past the car park (south-west) you can see **Winterburn Reservoir** in the valley. Taking the right-hand path at the T-junction (away from the car park) follow the clear track over **Boss Moor** for approximately ½ mile. When the path meets a gate, go through it and turn left in the direction of the **Malham Moor Lane** signpost. After 100 yards turn right before another gate at the signpost to **Skirethorns**.

5 The path now runs over **Threshfield Moor** to the right of a wire fence. Sections can again be quite boggy after rain. The fence meets a drystone wall where another signpost indicates the path then heads right, hugging the wall. Follow the wall until the footpath forks with the main path appearing to drift right. Take the narrower left-hand path that heads straight for another wall running in at a right angle from the right. A stile takes you through the wall and you can now see **Threshfield** and **Grassington** ahead. The path is clearly

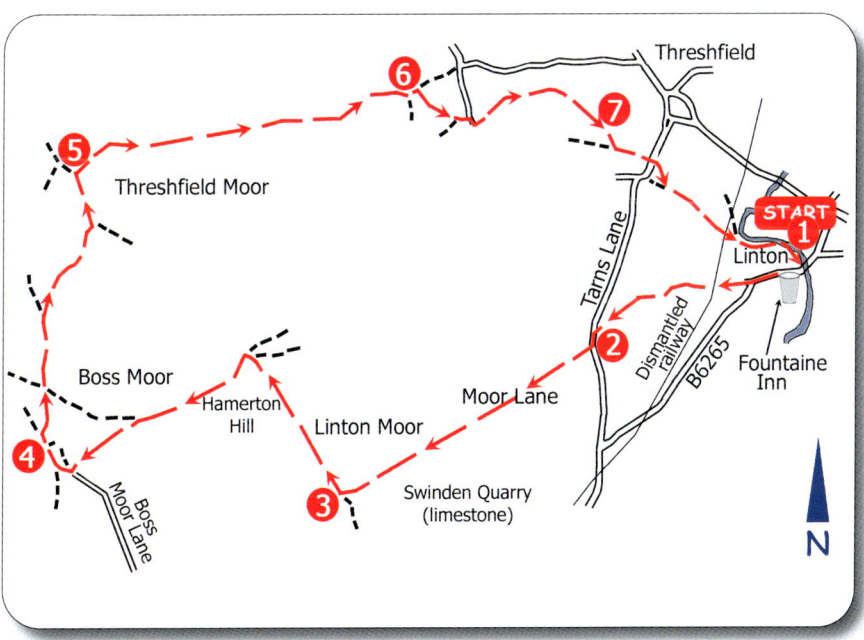

marked by yellow-painted wooden posts as it heads down through open fields and finally via a double wooden gate into hay meadows.

The path heads down towards a metal gate leading into a gravelled track with a 'Private Road' sign to the left (watch out for vehicles here). Turn right down the track passing **Lane House**, ignoring the first footpath to the right to **Boss Moor** but taking the second to the right to **Grysdale Lane**.

6 Cross a hay meadow leading to a wooden gate through a drystone wall next to two large ash trees. Go through the gate and take the path leading diagonally left towards a gate-less opening in the drystone wall. Keep in the same direction through this opening to the next gate in a drystone wall leading into a track heading downhill. After 50 yards, at the T-junction with **Grysdale Lane**, turn right (watch out for vehicles). After 70 yards turn left at the signpost to Threshfield, going over the stile into the field. Carry on down through a gap in a drystone wall to end up at a narrow stile by a larch tree. Go over the stone stile (this is quite narrow but there is a gate adjacent that can also be used) and down through the narrow field to a gated stile. Over the stile, follow the footpath across the flat field, crossing the track to **Gill House**, and then cross the footbridge over **Spiredale Beck** into the next field.

The footpath across this field is not obvious on the ground but head to the diagonal right-hand corner (easterly from the footbridge) to yet another stile. Go over this stile and keep right along the wall for 30 yards until another stile leads to an old path adjacent to a row of ash trees and old hawthorn bushes. Walk with the trees on your right up to a drystone wall. Once through the wall take the signed direction to the B6265 across the large field (in a south-easterly direction), where a bridge takes you over **Threshfield Beck**.

7 Crossing the bridge, look right to a spring where your dog can have a well deserved refreshing drink and a paddle. Turning left, keep to the field side as you now head towards the Grassington to Skipton road (the B6265). The exit from the field is visible as you approach the houses on your left. Go through the gate and down to the road. Cross the road with care to the footpath signed opposite. Through the gate turn half right and walk to the corner of the field. Go through the gateway, keeping the wall on your right. Ahead are trees and to the left the embankment of the old railway. Go through the trees into the next field. Cross this field diagonally, going down to an unusual stone bridge over the railway line, and once over keep heading down to the right-hand corner of the field. Go through the gate in the corner into **Well Lane**. This lane follows **Linton Beck** upstream to lead you into **Linton** itself, appearing at the side of the bridge on **Lauradale Road**. Now is the time to enjoy the delights of the village and relax in the **Fountaine Inn**.

11

Burnsall to Linton Falls

The fields around Burnsall.

This walk has a lot to recommend it, passing through lovely old field systems, surrounded with drystone walls. The last stage of the walk, alongside the River Wharfe, offers some interesting natural and man-made sights along the way, including Loup Scar limestone cliffs and St Michael and All Angels, a 12th-century church with 14th- and 15th-century extensions.

Burnsall is another picturesque Dales village in a lovely setting. The River Wharfe flows by it and a big lazy bend enfolds a large open space where many people set up their picnics in the summer. The old packhorse bridge in the centre was rebuilt in the 16th century and adds to the charming view from the green. 'Bonny Burnsall', as it is affectionately known, is well known for its canoeing competitions, tug of war and especially its annual Fell Race held every August. The race is one of the oldest on record with other games and sports going back to Elizabethan times. The village featured in the *Calendar Girls* film where it was used as the location for a fake Kilnsey Show – a bit odd as the setting for the real show is in a pretty setting already, just a few miles up the valley.

There is nothing demanding about this walk and the scenery is delightful throughout. Once you get to the Linton Falls the walk back alongside the Wharfe is especially relaxing and you can put your maps away and enjoy the ambience. Over the bridge at Linton Falls on the return stretch there will be more opportunities for your dog to be off its lead if you can trust it to keep out of the fast flowing river.

Terrain

Easy going along footpaths and farm tracks with no steep ascents/descents over the whole route.

Where to park

If you park considerately you can leave your car on the roadside in Burnsall, or use the car park in the village centre. **Sat nav:** BD23 6BW. However, it is very popular with tourists so get there early on summer weekends and bank holidays. **Maps:** OS Explorer OL2 Yorkshire Dales: South & West, Harvey Outdoor Yorkshire Dales: Dales South (GR SE032612).

How to get there

You can get to Burnsall from the east by following the B6160 from Bolton Abbey. Travelling north from Skipton on the B6265, turn right at the first Linton signpost just after passing Swinden Quarry. Follow this road through Linton, turning right onto the B6160 at the crossroads about ½ mile the other side of Linton. Follow this road down to Burnsall. Travelling south down Wharfedale take the Grassington signpost just opposite the garage at Threshfield. Turn almost immediately right (signpost to Burnsall B6160) and follow this all the way down to Burnsall.

Nearest refreshments

The Red Lion Hotel, Burnsall, welcomes dogs in the bar area, ☎ 01756 634542. www.redlion.co.uk

Dog factors

Distance: 5½ miles.
Road walking: Approximately 400 yards along Thorpe Lane and 200 yards on the side road leading to Fletcher Brow.
Livestock: Expect sheep in the fields around Burnsall.
Stiles: Plenty of these but all are gated or there is an adjacent gate.
Nearest vets: Kingsway Veterinary Group, Skipton.

The Walk

. . . .

① If you are starting on the village green, turn right to walk towards the **Red Lion** pub. Turn left up the road towards **Grassington** and a short distance after the sharp right-hand bend look out for the public footpath sign to **Thorpe**. Turn up the narrow passage that leads to a stile to go across several fields. Just after the second field there is a farm track with a wire fence on the opposite side that has a simple two-step stile where your dog might need a hand. At the time of writing the wire fence to the right could be lifted up to allow a dog to squeeze through. Fortunately, all the drystone wall boundaries on the rest of the walk can be crossed via gated stiles so should be no problem for you or your dog. For the next few fields the path is running close to some overhead power lines and follows roughly the same direction. Eventually the path goes under the power lines and starts to rise as it turns right along a wire fence going uphill. A few yards after the fence meets a drystone wall, a gated stile leads you into another field going up and over the hill. The path is now heading down towards **Badger Lane** (a farm track) which it crosses via a gate and then a stile opposite.

② The path is now a broad green track that rises up towards and between two large trees. At this point the track levels out and you can see ahead **Kail Hill**

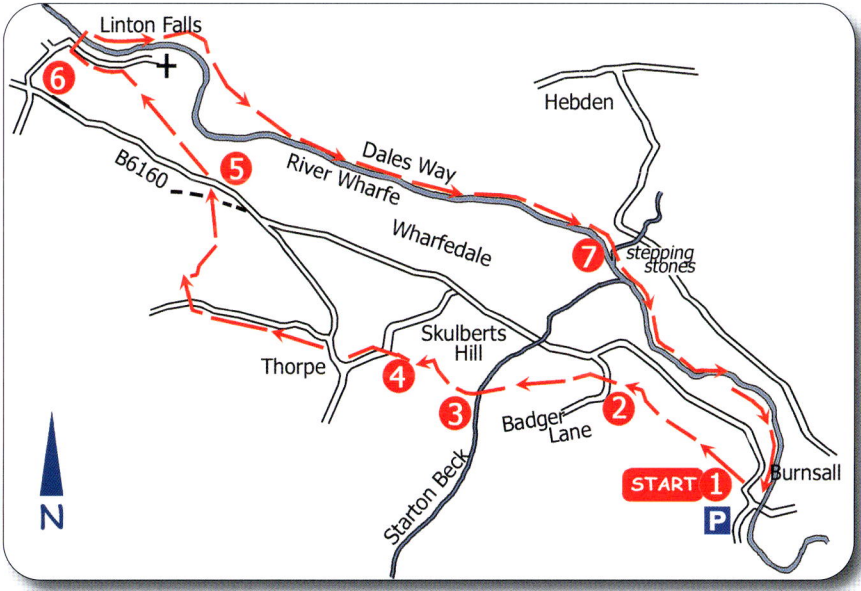

with **Thorpe village** hidden behind it. Carry on the track as it follows the contours before dropping down through two drystone walls to meet and go over **Starton Beck**.

3 The path now rises up again as it takes you into the field and heads along the wall and round past a small copse on the side of **Skulberts Hill**. Going through a wooden gate the path leads onto a gravelled track. Turn right and go up the track until it curves sharply left around the end of a drystone wall. The grassy lane ahead has walls on either side and you follow this all the way to a tarmac road.

4 Turn left along the road and follow it down into **Thorpe**. At the centre of the village turn right and follow the road out and up the hill. After about 75 yards take the lane to the left (**Thorpe Lane**) that continues to climb up. Eventually the road levels out and after about 200 yards there is a signpost for a bridleway to the B6160. Follow this sign down a narrow lane with drystone walls on either side. When the lane runs out at a gate, turn sharp left and walk by the side of the remains of a drystone wall. When these remains disappear,

The Linton Falls.

turn left again and you should see a gate in the drystone wall with a signpost next to it. Walk over to this and then through the gate, walking down to the bottom left-hand corner of the field (ignore the gated stile in the wall on the way down). Go through the gate and cross the B6160, heading right for a few yards until a footpath sign to **Linton Falls** shows you the path to take.

5 Walk across the two narrow fields and then into a much larger one where the path runs near the edge of an embankment overlooking the **River Wharfe**. Soon **St Michael and All Angels' church** comes into view by the side of the river. Continue on and through a gate to the right of a stone barn. Bear right across this last field towards the back of a house and then through a gate into a narrow lane between drystone walls. This quickly leads you down to a tarmac road where you turn left (or right if you want a short detour to visit the church). Walk on past a car park with public toilets on your left and past a few houses until you see a footpath sign to **Linton Falls** on the right. Follow the path round and onto the bridge over the **Wharfe**. After rain the falls below the bridge make an impressive sight.

6 If you go straight over the bridge and up away from the river, the path leads into the **Yorkshire Dales car park and visitor centre** (including public toilets), from where it's a short walk into Grassington where there are plenty of cafés and pubs for refreshments.

Turning right at the end of the bridge you will see the signpost showing you the path down to **Hebden** and **Burnsall**. Follow this footpath as it stays alongside the **River Wharfe** for most of the way back. Go first across three fields with the last leading via a gate onto a tarmac road. Turn right down this road and go past the trout farm and on to the **Dales Way** footpath to **Burnsall**. Turn left along the path through the broad flat field, crossing a small wooden footbridge along the way. A gate at the end of the field leads you to the path running alongside the **Wharfe**. The river is not fenced and can be very fast-flowing at times, so keep a watchful eye on your dog.

7 Eventually the path leads you to the suspension bridge and stepping stones over the river. When the river is high the stones are covered and the only way across is via the suspension bridge. This is a small challenge for people with vertigo; it's something I suffer from too but I manage it if I grit my teeth and, of course, hang on tight. Once on the other side of the river, turn left and follow the path all the way back to **Burnsall**. The path runs right up to the bridge at **Burnsall** and you can turn right here to get back up to the **Red Lion**.

Round Thruscross Reservoir

Looking north across the reservoir from West End.

Thruscross Reservoir is set at the top of the Washburn valley. In its short length the valley hosts four reservoirs (Fewston, Swinsty and Lindley Wood are the others, going down the valley) before the river meets the Wharfe just below Otley. Once out of the woods surrounding the reservoir there is a real sense of open space with fine views over empty moors.

The village of West End was flooded when the reservoir was built although it was already largely derelict following the decline of the flax industry. The remains of a flax mill are passed on the walk, and more of the village is revealed at times of drought. The reservoir wall is a large concrete structure but is very imposing when water overflows the spillway, creating an impressive waterfall crashing into the river below. A very conveniently placed bench in the middle of the walk offers the best place to sit with a hot flask and sandwiches and contemplate the world whilst looking out over the broad expanses of Pock Stones Moor.

There are lots of off-the-lead opportunities on this walk. Most of the paths by the side of the reservoir are completely safe for dogs and parts of the moorland too. Because of all the streams crossed and the reservoir itself there is not much need to carry extra water for your dog.

Dog factors
. . . .

Distance: 4¾ miles.
Road walking: Just 200 yards on a quiet lane.
Livestock: Sheep in the fields and cattle, too, around Whitmoor Farm.
Stiles: Several of these but all except one have a gate for dog access.
Nearest vets: Kingsway Veterinary Group, Skipton.

Terrain
Footpaths and wide tracks around the reservoir. One or two of the sections can get waterlogged after rain, so waterproof footwear is recommended. Short steep ascents/descents in a couple of places (less than 100 yards anywhere).

Where to park
There is a free car park adjacent to the reservoir. **Sat nav:** HG3 4BB. **Map:** OS Explorer 297 Lower Wharfedale & Washburn Valley (GR SE153573).

How to get there
Travelling from Otley take the B6451 out over the River Wharfe. Ignore the right-hand turn just after the bridge and follow the road as it climbs out of Otley into open country. After about 7 miles where the road meets the A59, cross the slightly staggered junction into Hall Lane. After about 1½ miles turn right down Reservoir Road. The car park is a further ¼ mile on the right just before the reservoir wall. Travelling from the east or west along the A59 look out for the crossroads at Blubberhouses.

Nearest refreshments
The Devonshire Arms Hotel at Bolton Abbey serves food and welcomes dogs in the lounge area, ☎ 01756 718111. www.devonshirehotels.co.uk

The Walk
. . . .

❶ Starting in the car park, go to the main drive-in entrance and cross the road to enter the wood. This wide path follows the edge of the reservoir for the next couple of miles before emerging alongside a minor road. In very dry weather if the water level is low enough you may even see the ruins of the drowned village of **West End**, sacrificed in the 1960s in order to build the reservoir. The old roadway down to the village still exists and the path crosses it on its way round. After the old roadway the path continues round the water's edge, running past the ruins of an old flax mill.

2 Where the path emerges by the road at the bottom of **Duke's Hill** follow it down to the footbridge over **Capelshaw Beck**. Cross over and turn left to go up onto the road. At the road turn right uphill until it levels out by a cattle grid on the right.

3 Go round the cattle grid into the lane to **Whitmoor Farm**. At the end of the first field a footpath sign indicates the path to follow on the left against a drystone wall. Follow close to the wall to the stile in the field corner. Go over this and turn left to keep close to the next wall until a gate and stile is reached. Either go through the gate or over the stile (this can be tricky as it has a metal bar across it that can make it difficult for medium-sized dogs to get past). This next field is often wet and covered in clumps of marsh grasses but the rutted

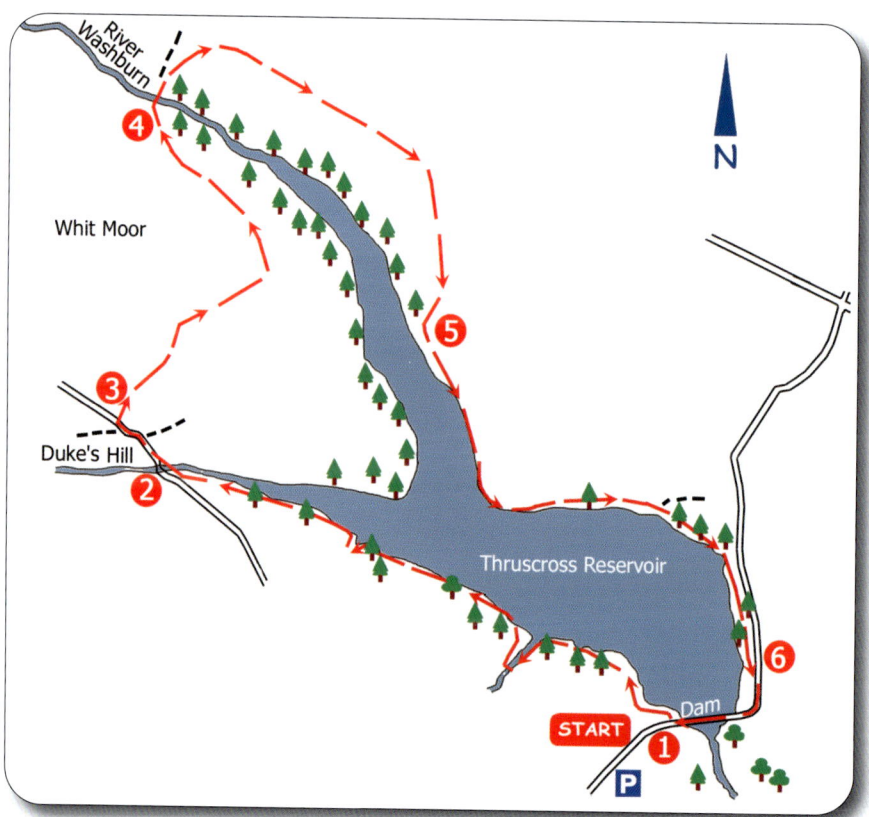

path at least is easy to follow. The path heads diagonally down towards the trees before bearing left to run parallel with them. Soon a ladder stile confronts you but there is a top-hinged 'gate' for your dog to get under just to the right of the stile. The path now continues on towards the edge of the wood and a convenient bench where you can sit and admire the views of the open moorland ahead (and have that hot drink from your flask). Below in the valley is the **River Washburn** just before it runs into the back of the reservoir.

The view from the track near Whitmoor Farm.

4 Follow the path on the steps down to the footbridge over the young Washburn river. A short steep, stepped path heads up the other side, keeping to the outside of the plantation. Once on the top there is now a very pleasant level walk across open moorland and you can get a good view of the main reservoir opening up ahead and to the right. Eventually the path swings to the left and down towards the edge of the plantation. A stile with a dog gate leads into a damp path between a drystone wall and the edge of the trees.

5 When you come to the bottom of the trees, turn right to follow the path overlooking an arm of the reservoir. This section can be very wet and boggy although a boardwalk helps you over some of it. Follow the path now as it heads towards the reservoir wall. It will drop down to run along the edge of the water and if your dog likes to swim, it will no doubt take this opportunity for a soak. The path runs up to a footbridge and into a scrubby area that has been recently felled and replanted with trees. The path bends around and eventually runs to **Reservoir Road** when it emerges from some older trees.

6 Now it's a road walk with your friend on a lead as you go over the top of the reservoir wall with an impressive view down the **Washburn Valley**. On the other side of the wall a footpath on the left takes you down and then back up to the car park.

Middleham & the River Cover

Taking a dip in the River Cover.

Situated on the southern slopes of Wensleydale, Middleham has a surprisingly large castle that was once the home of Richard III. The imposing castle ruins are well worth a look around (where your dog is also welcome, by the way). This is also a horse riding town with several well used bridleways and a practice horse racing track to the west. The recently inaugurated Six Dales Trail starts (or ends) at Middleham, leading eventually to the town of Otley in Wharfedale, 38 miles away.

The very attractive township is built under the dominating ruins of the 'haunted' castle. This walk runs by the eastern side of the castle out of the town and leads first down to the River Cover. Following this river upstream through some wild flower meadows you enjoy extensive views along Coverdale towards the ruins of Coverham Abbey, as well as Braithwaite Moor opposite.

Dog factors

Distance: 3½ miles.
Road walking: 200 yards on a footpath separated from the road by a wide grass verge.
Livestock: Grazing sheep and cattle may be in any of the fields.
Stiles: No difficult stiles on the whole route.
Nearest vets: Yoredale Vets, Leyburn.

Terrain
Short steep ascents/descents in a couple of places (less than 30 yards anywhere).

Where to park
There is a large free car park in the centre of Middleham. **Sat nav:** DL8 4PE. **Maps:** OS Explorer OL30 Yorkshire Dales: North & East, Harvey Outdoor Yorkshire Dales: Dales North (GR SE127877).

How to get there
From the south take the A6108 from Ripon via Masham. From the north the A684 runs from Bedale to Leyburn into Swaledale. The turning for Middleham is just to the east of Leyburn where you join the A6108.

Nearest refreshments
The friendly Richard III Hotel overlooks the market square in Middleham and welcomes dogs. Check the website for opening times. ☎ 01969 623240. www.richard111hotel.co.uk

The Walk

1 Starting from the centre of the main car park facing the **Dante**, turn right and walk up until you see an alleyway on your left. Take this and cross **Back Street** to continue up **Canaan Lane** with the castle now on your right. About 20 yards before the track ends at a gate turn left onto a footpath running between high hedges. Follow this path as it leads you out into a small rectangular field (walk along the left-hand side), through a squeeze stile and into a large open field that heads downhill towards **Straight Lane**. The OS map shows a footpath bearing right but that exit from the field is closed off now. Go down

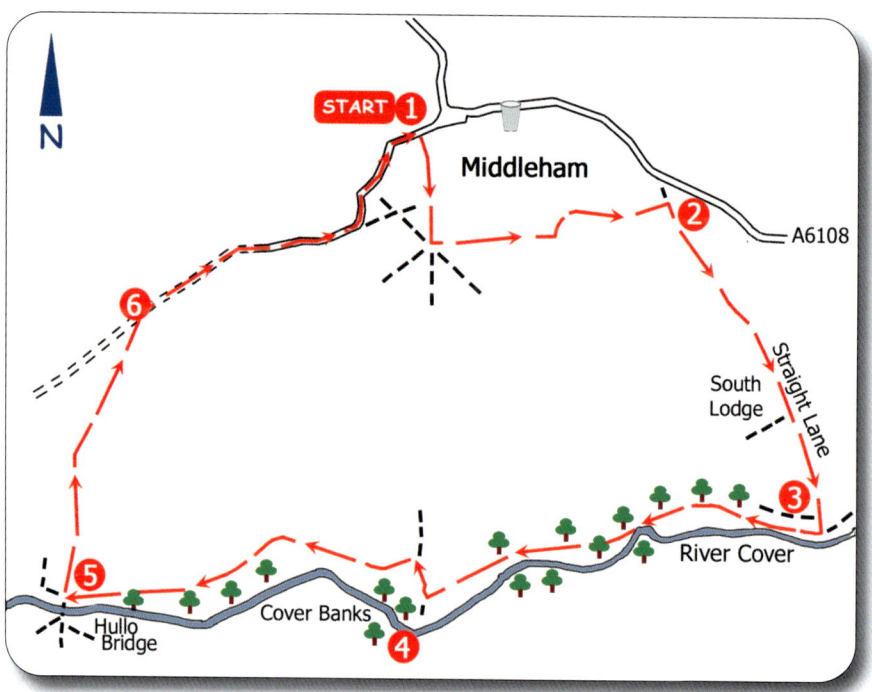

the hill heading for the left-hand corner and you will run up to the drystone wall boundary where a stile lets you into **Straight Lane**.

2 This lane, although quiet, is frequented by cars so the dog is safer on a lead along it. Turn right and follow the lane for several hundred yards until it turns sharp right (up to **South Lodge**). Ignore the right turn and carry straight on up to and through a gate into another large field. Keeping close to the right-hand drystone wall, follow the same direction until you drop down towards the **River Cover**.

3 Turn right where the field meets the river to follow the footpath on the bank side. There are some attractive stepping stones crossing the river where your best friend might like a paddle (but don't cross over yourself). You can now follow the clear riverside path as it leads you first through trees and then into some very pleasant open meadows that abound with wild flowers in spring and early summer. At the end of the second larger meadow the path leads you uphill away from the river. You can continue a little way along the river bank to a very pleasant picnic spot just where the path peters out. Here there are some big flat stones to sit on, almost in the river.

4 Back on the main route away from the river, at the top of the bank you should see a footpath (not always clearly defined here) that runs alongside a tree-edged boundary overlooking the river. Follow the field edge until you meet a stile taking you through the last corner of the trees via another stile into a large open field that slopes gently downhill ahead of you. The path runs through this field heading left towards the river again. Go through the trees and the path runs up to a stile with three footpath arrows on it.

5 If you go left, you are upon **Hullo Bridge** with very pleasant views up and down the river. Our path actually requires us to turn right and hug the boundary to our right as it makes up the hill. This path is indistinct for a while but if you keep to the right-hand boundary wall the way becomes clearer. Keep going up until a gate in the wall allows you into another field. Cross this field bearing diagonally left, still heading up the slope. As the field broadens out, head for the top right-hand corner where a stile leads you to the Coverham to Middleham road, where you turn right.

6 Even though there is a wide verge between the footpath and the road, it is still a good idea to have your four-legged friend on a lead here. Across the road you will see the training racecourse (the 'Gallop') that covers a large part of **Middleham Low Moor**. Soon **Middleham** itself comes into view and a gate on the right leads us back into fields. Through the gate, turn left to walk by the drystone wall towards and through another gate. Keeping alongside the wall, continue heading gently downhill. As the ground begins to level out you can see the back of the castle and there are now several paths across the fields to lead you back into **Canaan Lane** and the start of the walk.

Charlie still wet after his swim.

Bolton Castle & Aysgarth Falls

Admiring the falls.

Castle Bolton stands as a major landmark in the middle of Wensleydale and is the starting point of this delightful walk. Completed in 1399 by Sir Richard Le Scrope, at the time Lord Chancellor of England, Mary, Queen of Scots was imprisoned here in 1569, and it was besieged during the Civil War in 1645. The route leads on to Carperby whose claim to fame is the Wheatsheaf Hotel where Mr and Mrs Alf Wight, the former better known as James Herriot, the author who brought international fame to the Yorkshire Dales, honeymooned in 1941. As well as passing through the picturesque village of Carperby, the route leads you close to all three of the Aysgarth Falls along the River Ure. After rain the falls are pretty impressive and a popular tourist attraction. By the higher falls there are picnic tables too, so it's a good place to have your sandwiches and a drink and admire the views.

There are two awkward stiles to negotiate near the start but then it is pretty dog-friendly all the way. There are several small streams to cross, so a paddle is in order too.

Dog factors

Distance: 6 miles.
Road walking: About 50 yards either side of the car park at Aysgarth.
Livestock: Look out for grazing sheep in the fields.
Stiles: Plenty of these but all are gated or there is an adjacent gate, with the exception of two awkward stiles at the start of the walk.
Nearest vets: Bainbridge Vets, Station Surgery, Askrigg.

Terrain

A seriously muddy track approaching Carperby, but otherwise it is easy going.

Where to park

There is a rather expensive car park adjacent to Bolton Castle but the money is deducted from the castle entrance fee if you want to pay a visit. **Sat nav:** DL8 4ET. If you are considerate you can often find free parking places in the village itself. **Maps:** OS Explorer OL30 Yorkshire Dales: North & East, Harvey Outdoor Yorkshire Dales: Dales North (GR SE032918).

How to get there

Travelling from the east up Wensleydale, take the road to Grinton and Reeth out of Leyburn. At the crossroads before Bellerby Camp turn left towards Redmire. After the road starts to drop down from Redmire Scar turn right and follow the lane all the way into Castle Bolton.

Nearest refreshments

The Wheatsheaf Hotel, Carperby. As well as its connection with James Herriott, in January 1942, Greta Garbo stayed here following an evening entertaining troops at Catterick Garrison, with Henry Hall, the band leader. So there's a good enough reason to stop there yourself, ☎ 01969 663216. www.wheatsheafinwensleydale.co.uk

The Walk

1 The route starts at the back of the castle where the footpath is signposted to **Aysgarth** just before the car park entrance. Cross the field diagonally and exit via a small gated stile into the next small wooded field. Cross this and through the stile head into a much larger field heading slightly down, passing

Yorkshire Dales – A Dog Walker's Guide

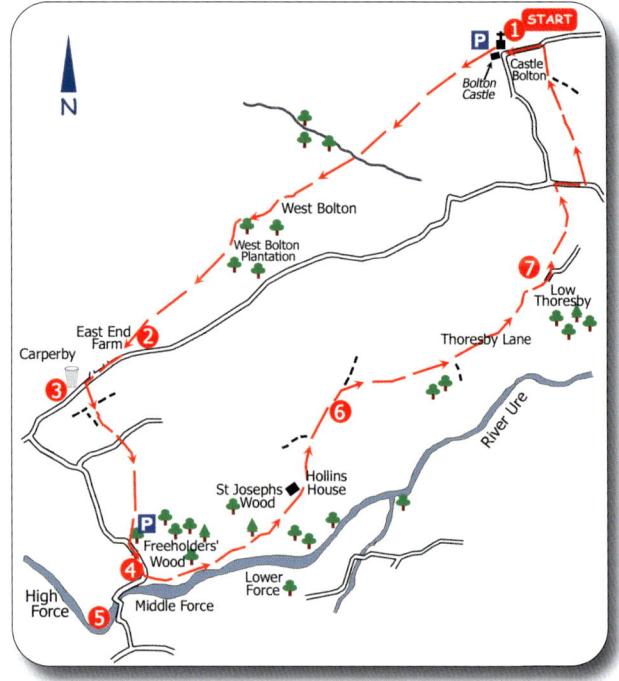

Your dog may need a hand over this. Cross the next field bearing left to cross a similar step-stile over the wire fence. Luckily this is the last (at the time of writing) difficult stile to get over and your dog should still be clean and dry.

Walk on towards a line of trees in a small gully ahead. As you drop down into the gulley cross over the stream (**Beldon Beck**) and turn right up to a gated stile. Through the stile you can see the hamlet of **West Bolton** ahead. Follow the path as it heads towards it and then onto a track in front of the farm buildings. Just past the buildings turn right off the track on a path that leads up and round the mound of trees of **West Bolton Plantation**. A signpost then indicates the way onwards to **Carperby**, the path first leading you over two small stone slab bridges before passing by a small pond on the right. A series of fields are crossed as you head towards **Carperby**. The track now gets very muddy after wet weather and care is needed on the last section as it heads down to **East End Farm**. Look out for the footpath on the left leading through a messy, overgrown field and onto the road.

② Turn right and head into the village. You pass the **Wheatsheaf** pub on the way through the village.

③ Turn left at the signpost for **Aysgarth**, where the path leads you through a number of small fields all bounded by drystone walls. Luckily, gated stiles are the norm so it's just a matter of following the signs towards **Aysgarth**. Eventually the path leads into the **Freeholders' Wood Nature Reserve** and then down to the Aysgarth to Carperby road. Turn left here and head downhill and under the (disused) railway bridge.

4 To view the **High Aysgarth Falls** turn right up to the National Park car park and walk through it. Follow the signs to the falls where there are also benches where you can eat your sandwiches and have a drink with the falls nearby. There is a café in the car park but sadly it does not allow dogs inside.

5 Returning and continuing the walk, about 20 yards after the car park take the footpath on the left of the road into **Freeholders' Wood** and to the middle and lower falls. There is a very short detour to the right of the path down to a viewing point for the **Middle Force falls**. Later as the path heads on to **St Joseph's Wood**, at a fork in the path, you can either go straight on to take a look at the lower falls (returning to the same place), or take the left-hand way directly back to **Castle Bolton**. The path then leads away from the wood towards **Hollins House** where it runs into a broad track round the buildings. Follow the track for a short distance until you see a signpost to the right. This path heads towards **Thoresby**. At the next signpost take the path across a large field directed to **Low Thoresby**. At the other side of the field another signpost in front of a gated stile shows the way to **Thoresby Lane**.

6 Turn right at the stile, now ignoring the direct path to **Castle Bolton**. Head along the wall towards and through the gate. The next field can be boggy after rain but keep close to the wall and head on in the same direction into a second field (passing a sign to Castle Bolton on the way). At the time of writing the second field was being fenced off; walk alongside the new fencing and through the gate into **Thoresby Lane**. Walk along the lane all the way to **Low Thoresby** and turn left where the lane meets the houses and left again to lead onto a bridge over the beck.

7 Take a footpath to the left a short distance across the end of a field to a second signpost where you turn right. The path now follows the hedge and drystone wall until the field widens, where it then heads for the top right corner (to the left of some old outbuildings). Go through the gate and head across the long narrow field to the road. The castle is clearly visible up the hill now. At the road turn right and walk down it for about 150 yards until a signpost to **Bolton Castle** shows a way through to the fields on the left. After going through four drystone walls head diagonally left in the next field and look out for a narrow stile to take you on to the other side of the wall. Keep heading up and the path now leads to the small cutting of the now disused **Wensleydale railway** line. Cross this and head directly up through the next three fields and the path eventually emerges back in **Castle Bolton**.

West Burton & Three Falls

Below Cauldron Falls near West Burton.

West Burton is a typical Dales village built around a large open green, edged with a few shops and a dog-friendly pub. In the centre of the green is an ancient market cross and with several benches round the side, this is a very pleasant location to sit and watch the world go by. The Walden Beck runs in a narrow valley on the eastern side of the village and after rain the Cauldron Falls are an impressive sight. Turner visited West Burton on 28 July 1816, as part of his grand tour of Yorkshire. He made a famous pencil sketch of the falls, which can be seen on the Tate online website.

On the way out the route crosses pleasant meadows and eventually runs alongside both the Aysgarth Middle and Lower Forces on the River Ure. There are several good spots alongside the river to eat your sandwiches and admire the view. The return journey leads up onto the lower slopes of West Witton moor and gives some fine views before dropping back down into West Burton via the Cauldron Falls.

Dog factors

Distance: 5 miles.
Road walking: From Hestholme Bridge you have to walk about 300 yards to Temple Farm on the A684.
Livestock: Sheep and cattle grazing in the fields.
Stiles: There are plenty of stiles along the way but nearly all are gated, with none being difficult to get over.
Nearest vets: Bainbridge Vets, Station Surgery, Askrigg.

Terrain

A few short steep ascents/descents but nothing very strenuous.

Where to park

There is lots of parking around the village green at West Burton. **Sat nav:** DL8 4JY. **Maps:** OS Explorer OL30 Yorkshire Dales: North & East, Harvey Outdoor Yorkshire Dales: Dales North (GR SE016866).

How to get there

Coming from Wensleydale, turn off the A684 onto the B6160 between Aysgarth and West Witton. Turn left into the village after approximately 1 mile.

Nearest refreshments

At the Fox and Hounds Inn, West Burton, dogs are allowed in the bar but not the restaurant (but the same food is served in each room), ☎ 01969 663111. www.foxandhoundswestburton.co.uk

The Walk

1 From the village green head towards the post office and the **Fox and Hounds** pub on **Greenview**. Walk past the post office and tea room away from the pub down **Back Nook** for about 200 yards. Take the footpath on the left signed for **Eshington Bridge**. This leads you down to and across the B6160 as it heads up **Bishopdale**.

2 Continue directly across the first field, passing to the left of an old barn into a second field when you need to head diagonally right into the corner. Go through the gate and cut across the corner of another field before turning

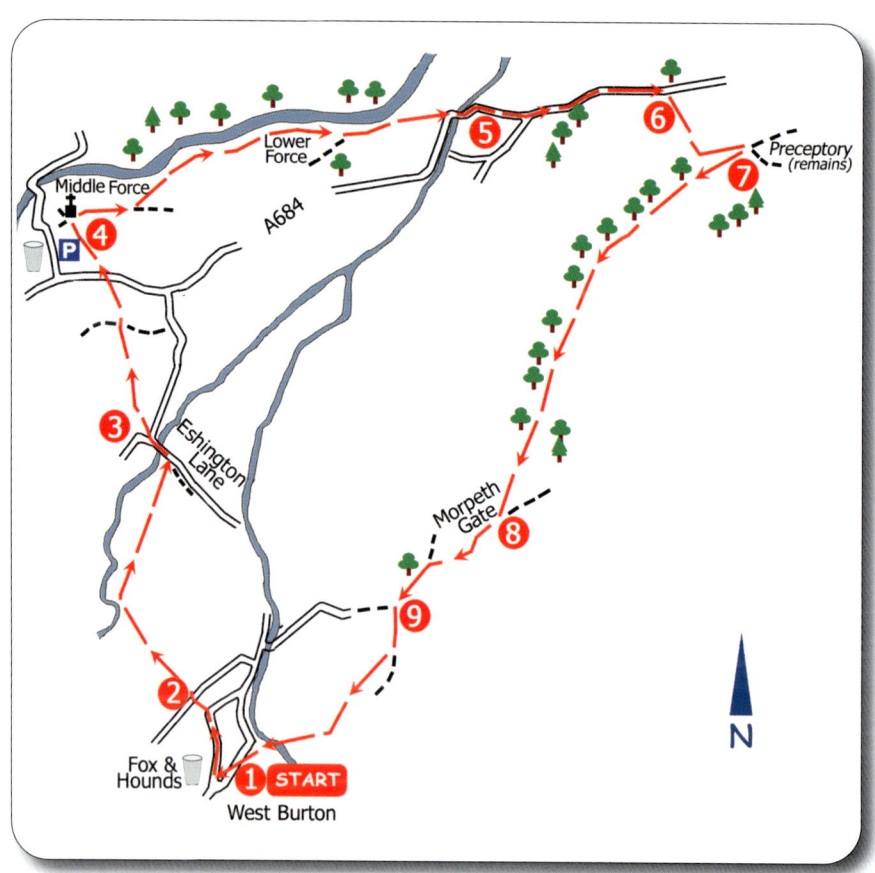

stile onto **Eshington Lane**. Turn left to go over the bridge and then follow the road right.

3 Immediately a signpost indicates the footpath to **Palmer Flatts** (an unknown location on the map!). Go through the wall and climb up behind the power line pole to go through a narrow stile, then immediately turn right to go through into another two fields to a wooden gate. Go on through the gate following the drystone wall on your right up to and through another gate. You will now be overlooking a small dry valley and can see the path to follow down and up the other side. Pass through the gate and cross the field ahead to get to the A684. Cross the road and into the lane opposite (signpost to **Yore Bridge**). Walk down this lane and into the churchyard on your right, then round the church and follow the footpath out again.

4 Follow the path across a small field up to and into a small copse. On emerging from the copse, keep left along the field edge. You will be able to hear the noise of **Aysgarth Middle Force** to your left and see it once you have reached and passed through the next gate. Keep close to the river, following the path via a couple of wooden gates onto and past the **Lower Force**. After the falls the path pulls away from the river to head across three fields before meeting the A684 again at **Hestholme Bridge** over **Bishopdale Beck**.

5 At the roadside turn left and tramp up the road for about 300 yards. Keep on the verge when you can as the traffic can sometimes be travelling quite fast. Keep on the road until you see the signposts for the **Templars Chapel** and **Morpeth Gate** on your right.

6 Going into the field, keep to the left and climb up towards the woods. The path leads into a lane (that always seems to be wet and muddy) cutting up through the wood to emerge on a wide grassy shelf.

7 Turn right through the stile and go into the field in the direction of **Morpeth Gate**. This broad level shelf is our route for the next ¾ mile, passing through stone walls and wide fields with springs emerging along the way. Look out for the occasional elm tree still clinging on to life here on the edge of the wood to your left. After two more gated stiles and then crossing two crumbled drystone walls, look out for a wooden gate down to the right. This is the path to follow just below the shelf and at first is not very distinct but further on becomes more obvious. A metal gate ahead leads you into **Morpeth Gate**, a track heading out of **West Burton** up onto **Morpeth Scar**.

8 Once in the lane head downhill, first passing a sign on your right for **Temple Farm** and then taking the next signed path on your left (about 70 yards further on) to **West Burton** via **Barrack Wood**. The last sign is quite well hidden and easy to miss. If you have come to an open field on your left with a large ash tree by the gate, you have come too far!

9 Following the rough path to **Barrack Wood**, turn down diagonally to the right, to cross the field and go through narrow stiles into a second then a third field. Keep more or less in a straight line and only turn right when you run up to a signpost indicating **West Burton** is to your right (with Barrack Wood and Cote Bridge signed as well). The path downhill is well-trodden now and leads through two wooden gates before turning into woods growing around **Walden Beck**. Follow the path down to the beck and if you turn left you will see the **Cauldron Falls**. The route back to the village green continues right, then over the bridge to head right again between the buildings, finally turning left at the road junction to head up to the green.

Bainbridge, Worton & Askrigg

Waterfalls on the River Bain.

Starting in Bainbridge, this round trip first takes you above the site of the Roman fort of Virosidum. This fort was at one end of the Cam High Road, a Roman road connecting Bainbridge to Ingleton (a section of which is crossed on the Burtersett walk). The foundations cover an area of more than 1½ acres, and Bainbridge was an important road centre in Roman times. The village is built around a surprisingly large green, including ancient stocks and shady trees.

The villages of Worton and then Aysgarth are visited in turn and in between there are many very pleasant footpaths to walk. Just before Askrigg the footpath goes across the disused Wensleydale railway line that used to run from Northallerton on the main East Coast main line to Garsdale on the Settle to Carlisle route. The name Askrigg is of Old Norse origin, meaning 'the ridge where ash trees grow', denoting the existence of Viking settlers and their farming. The oldest settlement probably dates back to the Iron Age. Askrigg

Dog factors

Distance: 4 miles.
Road walking: Short stretch from the Yore Bridge back into Bainbridge and a short section on the way out.
Livestock: Sheep grazing in most of the fields.
Stiles: Plenty of these but all are gated or there is an adjacent gate.
Nearest vets: Bainbridge Vets, Station Surgery, Askrigg.

farming. The oldest settlement probably dates back to the Iron Age. Askrigg itself is a charming place and has been used as the fictional Darrowby in the BBC series *All Creatures Great and Small*.

It's not a walk of wide open spaces, but there is plenty of scope to take off your dog's lead if there are no farm animals about. The walk after Worton is 'dry' so it would be advisable to carry some water on a hot day.

Terrain

A quite steep but short climb up to and back down from Brough Scar.

Where to park

There are lots of parking places around the green in Bainbridge. **Sat nav:** DL8 3EW. **Maps:** OS Explorer OL30 Yorkshire Dales: North & East, Harvey Outdoor Yorkshire Dales: Dales North (GR SD933903).

How to get there

Bainbridge sits on the main A684 running through Wensleydale between Hawes (in the west) and Aysgarth (in the east).

Nearest refreshments

The Rose and Crown Hotel, Bainbridge, DL8 3EE, ☎ 01969 650225. The Victoria Arms in Worton is just off the route but easy to find a little further down on the A684. Dogs are welcome both inside and in the large garden. ☎ 01969 650314. Virtually all the pubs and tea rooms in Askrigg welcome dogs too.

The Walk

1 From the green, head east out on the A684 towards **Aysgarth**. On the way take some time to have a look at the impressive falls on the **River Bain** just

outside the village. Turn right at the junction with the lane to **Low Force** and immediately take the footpath into the field on your left towards **Cubeck**. Walk across to the gate just to the right of the power line pole and then cross the next field in the same direction. On the top side wall there is a stile into the small field below the trees. Go into the small field and then head up the bank to the top left-hand corner. Before going into the next field look back and you can see the outline of the Roman fort of **Virosidum** on the other side of the main road.

2 Into the next field, follow the path along the left-hand wall as it runs along the contour of the broad shelf of **Brough Scar**. Soon the path runs up to woods and between them and several more fields. Various elm trees survive here, a very rare sighting elsewhere. Eventually the path runs up to a signpost indicating it is time to drop down towards **Worton** through the wood. The path is pretty wet at the base of the hill but dries out again once you are crossing the large field. Cross the field bearing down and right, heading towards the large gate in the lower right-hand corner against the road.

3 Cross the road (A684 again) and head right briefly before turning left into **Worton**. Walk down through the village towards the **River Ure**. Cross the

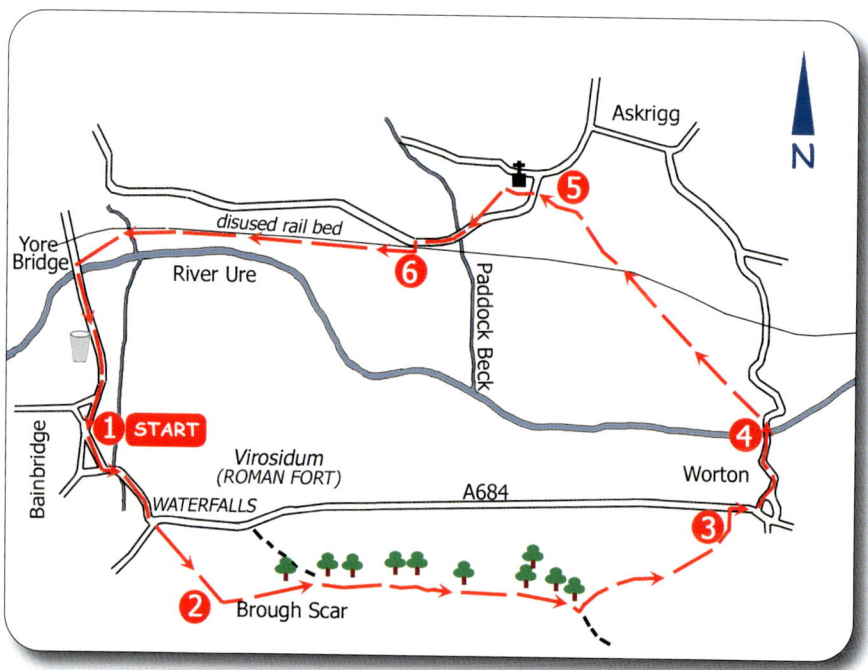

On the edge of Worton Scar.

river over **Worton Bridge** and turn left along the path signed for 'Askrigg ¾ mile'.

4 The following pathway is paved with large stone slabs as it leads across several fields up to the now disused railway line. Go up and onto the old rail bed, turning left and then right a few yards later. Go up the steps and on up the hill through a couple of gates into **Askrigg**. If ever there was a dog-friendly place it's Askrigg. There are several pubs and tea rooms, and dogs are welcome in some rooms at all of them. As the walk is two-thirds completed it might just be a good time for a break and refreshment.

5 Leave the village by walking through the churchyard and out the back past some cottages to drop down across two fields to gain the minor road to **Bainbridge**. Cross over and after the road goes over **Paddock Beck** turn left about 70 yards further on at the signpost to Yorbridge, ¾ mile.

6 Follow the track down to the old railway line and turn right (via either the large metal gate or over the small wooden stile) to walk along it. Keep alongside the line through four more fields and over **Grange Beck** before bearing left once again over a paved path towards **Yorbridge**, where you turn left onto the road back into **Bainbridge**.

Burtersett & Wether Fell

Looking back over Burtersett.

This is definitely a walk for a fine day, as the normally extensive views are easily blocked out by low cloud. Having said that, it is an exhilarating climb out of Burtersett with great views across Wensleydale. On top of Wether Fell is the summit known as Drumaldrace (614 metres). There is a trig point that you might want to visit and it is only a short detour off the route.

The main walk is on a broad track or grassy bridleway and is not only easy to follow to the top but safe for your dog too (but keep them under control where sheep are grazing). There used to be several stone quarries near Burtersett that were at their peak of production around 1890 and for many years after the opening of the Wensleydale railway around 15,000 tons of stone flags were sent from Hawes station every month, production ending in the 1930s. A highlight of the route is the walk along a section of Cam High Road on the path of the Roman road up from Bainbridge over to Ilkley. In 1751 it became part of the turnpike road from Richmond to Lancaster, only losing this role when Hawes took over from Askrigg as the major market town and the road was re-routed via Widdale. Sometimes there are mountain bikers using this road.

Terrain
It's a long haul up from Bainbridge, but worth it.

Where to park
There are several parking spaces along the roads in Burtersett village. **Sat nav:** DL8 3PQ. **Maps:** OS Explorer OL30 Yorkshire Dales: North & East, Harvey Outdoor Yorkshire Dales: Dales North (GR SD890892).

How to get there
Burtersett is just over a mile to the east of Hawes just off the main A684 through Wensleydale.

Nearest refreshments
The Board Inn, Market Place, Hawes, welcomes dogs inside. There is a cosy fire in the bar area and it serves home-cooked food ☎ 01969 667223.

The Walk
. . . .

1 Leaving the village centre head out via **Shaws Lane** (dead end), then turn left at the next opportunity up a signposted track. The track runs through a shallow ford where a stream comes in from the left – a good place for a refreshing splash for your friend. A gate ahead leads onto the main track that bends first right and then left as it makes its way up the hillside. The track is long and steep so take every opportunity to stop and look back over **Burtersett** and the surrounding valley. The track eventually makes its way to the right round the bulk of **Yorburgh**. When you are well above **Yorburgh** the track becomes greener as coarse grasses take over. Take the main (right) fork both times.

Dog factors
. . . .
Distance: 5¼ miles.
Road walking: None at all.
Livestock: Possibility of encountering sheep grazing.
Stiles: No difficult ones on this route.
Nearest vets: Bainbridge Vets, Station Surgery, Askrigg.

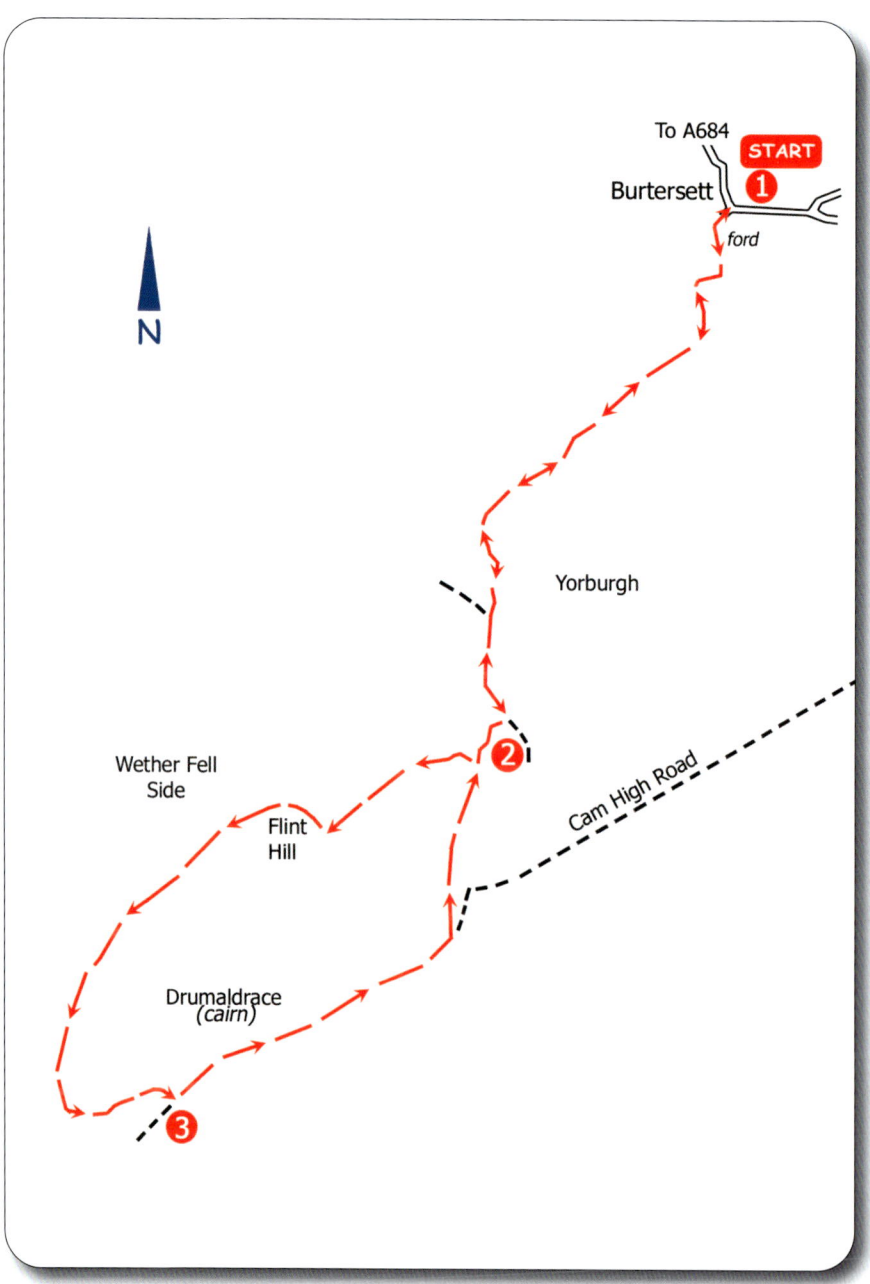

Part of the old Roman road.

2 The track more or less runs out at a gate in the fence. Go through the gate and head roughly right into a disused quarry area near **Flint Hill** with outcrops of limestone, making quite a good place for a break. The next section heading round the perimeter is pretty uneven and the path is not very distinct, particularly over eroded peat channels. There are great views over **Sleddale** here and over to **Hawes** if you are lucky with the weather. Keep near to the perimeter wall though and the route leads right around the **Drumaldrace top** to finally emerge on **Cam High Road** (an old Roman road) that heads downhill to **Bainbridge**. In clear weather there are wonderful views over **Marsett** and **Semer Water** over to the right in **Raydale**.

3 Turn left here to follow the path of the Roman road to the first bridleway sign to the left, indicating the route back down to point 2 and on to **Yorburgh** to retrace your steps back to **Burtersett**.

Upper Swaledale & Kisdon

Charlie waiting to descend to Muker.

This walk has plenty of variety from tranquil meadows to waterfalls and rugged hilltops with extensive views down Swaledale. Lead mining used to be a major part of the local economy and there is plenty of evidence of this around Swinner Gill with various ruins and waste screes. Muker is a very attractive village. Originally a Norse settlement, the name is derived from the Norse words *Mjor-aker* meaning 'the narrow acre'. The location at the meeting of the River Swale and the Straw Beck with the surrounding meadows is most likely why the Vikings chose to settle here. The very dog-friendly pub is called the Farmers Arms and there is also a village shop and post office, as well as craft shops and a café. Originally the vicarage, the teashop was built in 1680 and retains much of its 'olde worlde' charm today. Information about the National Park can be found at the Muker Village Store.

There are no difficult stiles to overcome and as long as you can keep close control of your dog when passing through meadows of grazing sheep, it is dog-friendly all the way. For the water-loving dog there are lots of opportunities for a paddle in the River Wharfe, as well as in many streams and springs.

Terrain

The second half of the walk involves a moderately steep ascent up the side of Kisdon Hill, followed by a similar descent at the end.

Where to park

There is a pay and display car park by the river and limited parking elsewhere in Muker if you are lucky (but be considerate). **Sat nav:** DL11 6QG. It is very popular with tourists so get there early on summer weekends and bank holidays. **Maps:** OS Explorer OL30 Yorkshire Dales: North & East, Harvey Outdoor Yorkshire Dales: Dales North (GR SD910978).

How to get there

Travelling from the east up Swaledale, Muker is on the main road (B6270) through the valley. You can also approach via Wensleydale over the Cliff Gate Road from Hawse. This is quite a challenging route in poor weather.

Nearest refreshments

In Muker there is the Farmers Arms, ☎ 01748 343130 and Muker Village Store & Tea Shop, ☎ 01748 886409. Both are dog friendly and will welcome your hound.

The Walk

....

1 As you leave the car park, turn left onto the main road to go over the river and follow the road until you can turn right, up into the village. Follow the tarmac lane and when it levels out, after about 75 yards, walk to the right of the building in front of you (it has iron railings on the wall and steps up to an entrance on its right end). Walking past this you will soon see the first footpath sign for **Gunnerside & Keld** pointing towards the rear of the village. This footpath will take you out of the village, through some attractive meadows, bordered by drystone walls, down to the **River Swale**. Initially the easy to follow path is rough gravel but then becomes paved with stone slabs. Each field boundary wall you cross is either gated or has an easy to negotiate stile. At the last stile before the river a signpost points left to **Keld** and right to **Gunnerside**. Take the right-hand direction to walk alongside the river towards and over the footbridge. On the other side of the footbridge go up the bank a few yards to another signpost and this time turn left in the direction of **Keld**.

Dog factors

Distance: 6 miles.
Road walking: Limited to the distance from the car park through Muker village to the first footpath.
Livestock: Expect to encounter sheep in the meadows.
Stiles: Plenty of these but all are gated or there is an adjacent gate.
Nearest vets: Swale Veterinary Surgery, Richmond.

2 The clear path soon broadens out into a wide gravelled track taking you right up the valley with the **River Swale** on your left all the way. If you have spent a few hours driving to Muker now might be a good time to find a big flat stone to sit on and eat your sandwiches by the side of the river, whilst your dog can have a good splash in the broad shallow bed. Carrying on up the valley you come to where **Swinner Gill** enters the **Swale**.

3 There are abandoned mine buildings running up the sides of the narrow valley. The work here was gruelling and dangerous but the area has a very peaceful air about it now. There are several small but attractive waterfalls along **Swinner Gill** too (a good place for your doggy friend to splash around again). Cross **Swinner Gill** via the footbridge and follow the track up and through the gate (ignoring the track heading down to the river on the left). This broad path leads you up to another gate and soon you pass the remains of **Crackpot Hall** on your right. It's perhaps worth a detour if you have the time to explore the ruins. Eventually the track levels out again and as you follow it round a stone barn on your left it starts to descend again. Going through a gate across the track follow it down until another gate leads you to the bridge over **East Gill**. This large stream drops down to the **Swale** over a number of attractive falls and is another good spot to have a picnic.

4 Follow the path to the left (now a section of the **Pennine Way**) as it goes down to a footbridge over the river. First go straight ahead and then right as the path climbs steeply for a short stretch before reaching a T-junction against a drystone wall. Turn left (again on the **Pennine Way**) and follow the path through some woods. Down the **Swale** from here is **Kisdon Force**, a series of falls that are impressive after rain. To get to the falls (a detour from our route), take the first left-hand path downhill (signposted Kisdon Upper Force). The path down can be very slippery when wet, so take care. You will be rewarded with a close-up of **Kisdon Force** as the **Swale** tumbles over two big steps in the underlying rock.

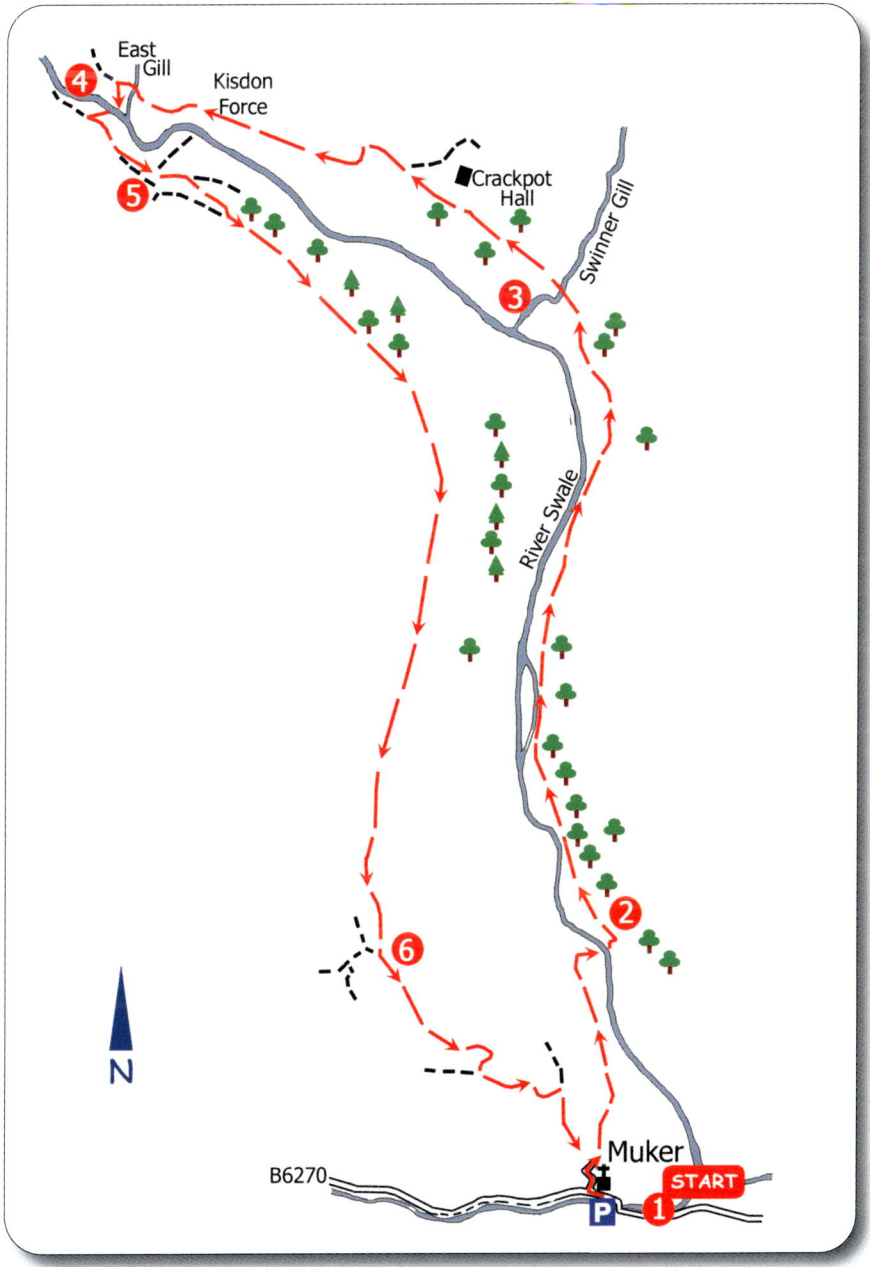

East Gill

Kisdon Force

Crackpot Hall

Swinner Gill

River Swale

Muker

START

B6270

N

5 Continuing on the main route, take the next right-hand path (signposted to Thwaite and Muker) up the hill. You could follow the more direct route down the valley side to **Muker** but the views are so much better going the higher (right-hand) route. As the path continues to rise, wide views over the valley below open out and the tumbledown drystone walls by the side of the path enhance the rugged feel. At the next signpost again take the left-hand direction along the **Pennine Way** that leads you on a narrow path just above the trees. Soon the path rises again and you emerge into a much more rugged landscape with the ruined wall to your left and the rock-strewn hill rising to your right.

The falls along Swinner Gill.

The views keep getting better as the path follows the contour round the hill top. Soon views down the main **Swaledale valley** open up as **Muker** comes into view again. The path continues more or less on a contour through three gated stiles and one small gate until you come to a small ladder stile. The ladder stile is over a low section of wall and should be no trouble to any dog. Over the stile bear left, from here the path starts heading downhill past a signpost and then on to a T-junction where you leave the **Pennine Way** and head down to **Muker** (now signed just ¾ mile away).

6 The very pleasant lane, bordered by drystone walls, ends at a gate leading into a gravelled lane. This can now be followed all the way down the hill back to the start.

19

Gunnerside Gill to Barf End

The view over to Jingle Pot Edge from Potting.

This very enjoyable walk takes you up a narrow valley beside Gunnerside Beck before returning via a higher route that gives rise to some great views over isolated farmhouses and hamlets. Gunnerside is home to the Old Working Smithy and Museum established in 1795 at the bottom of Gunnerside Gill which displays an interesting collection of objects amassed over the years. The Smithy is still worked by the sixth generation of blacksmiths in the Calvert family. Gunnerside Gill is a small valley running northwards, at right angles to the main Swale valley. This was the site of major lead mining until the late 19th century. All that's left now are some ruins and waste heaps that are partially overgrown and almost blend back into the landscape.

The broad track that runs below Winterings Scar to Barf End that is followed for a large part of the walk is ideal for dog walking. It's relatively safe except for the odd farm vehicle and passing mountain bike. Sections of it are unfenced so there are opportunities to paddle in streams and springs too.

Yorkshire Dales – A Dog Walker's Guide

Terrain

Some short, steep sections early in the walk.

Where to park

You should be able to find a parking place by the roads in Gunnerside village, if you are considerate. **Sat nav:** DL11 6LA. **Maps:** OS Explorer OL30 Yorkshire Dales: North & East, Harvey Outdoor Yorkshire Dales: Dales North (GR SD950982).

How to get there

Travelling from the east up Swaledale, Gunnerside is on the main road (B6270) through the valley. You can also approach via Wensleydale over the Cliff Gate Road from Hawse. This is quite a challenging route in poor weather.

Nearest refreshments

The Kings Head, Gunnerside. This friendly pub welcomes dogs and serves food. ☎ 01748 883412. www.kingsheadgunnerside.com

The Walk
. . . .

1 Assuming you are standing on the bridge over **Gunnerside Beck** in the middle of the village, go up the footpath on the right (signed Gunnerside Beck) following the beck (on your left-hand side) upstream. The path is quite steep and narrow in places, sometimes running right next to the beck and other times up amongst the tree, but always heading upstream. In the woods you are likely to see forget-me-nots and wild garlic in late spring/early summer and if you are lucky, roe deer, too. Eventually the path drops down, leaving the **Birkbeck woods** behind, where a footbridge (railway sleeper) takes you over a small beck before the valley floor widens out. Continue up the valley via two stiles and a gated stile to reach the remains of the buildings housing the 'Sir Francis Dressing Floor' where lead ore was sorted and crushed before smelting.

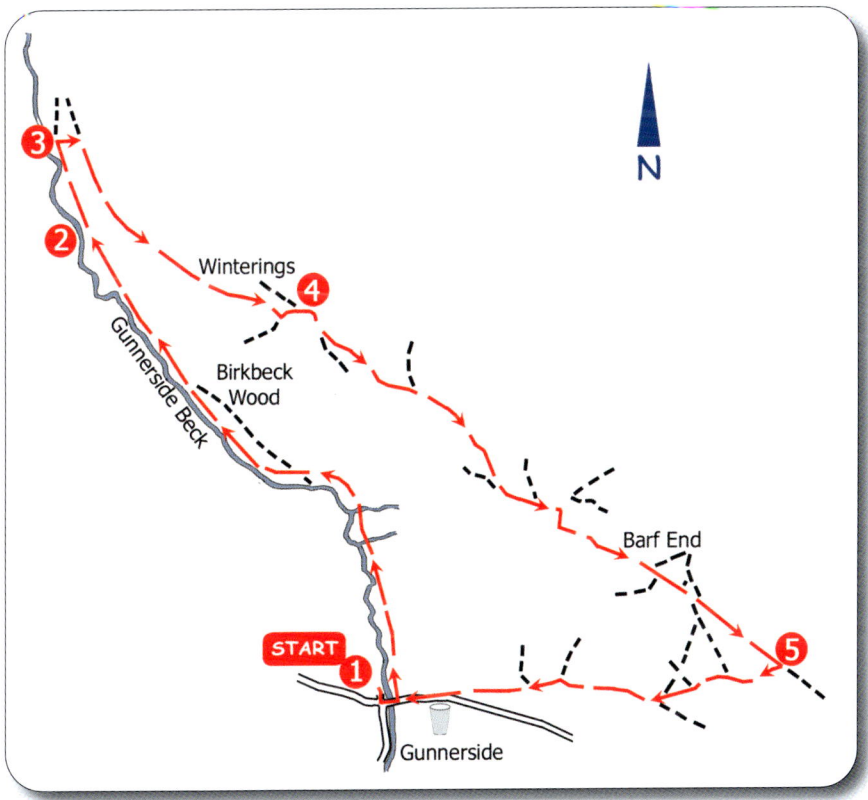

2 Walking past the ruins on your right, a yellow-topped post indicates the location of a wooden stile. Go over the stile and walk on to a second stile where the path starts to gently climb up. After the second stile the path leads up to and through a drystone wall and into more open bracken covered fields.

3 Approximately 150 yards on, the path is crossed by another coming up the hill. Turn right here and head up, climbing for a while and heading back in the direction of **Gunnerside**. Soon the path meets and goes through a series of drystone walls. You might just meet mountain bikers from here onwards so keep your dog close by to avoid any collisions. The path occasionally seems to disappear but as long as you don't go down you will pick it up again as it hugs different sides of the drystone walls. Where you go through a stile with two large vertical stones on either side, the path enters a large field that becomes rock-strewn and has a short section of drystone wall standing alone in the middle of it. Go round the top (left) side of this wall and head left

A shady path through the woods.

and up as you eventually come to another drystone wall. On your left you should now see a wide green track with a wire fence by the side. Head towards this and turn right along it. This area is shown as the **Winterings** on the OS map.

4 The next leg of the walk is a nice, easy stroll along this track as it runs roughly on a contour on the valley side with some lovely views over **Swaledale**. About ¾ mile along the track, look out for a gate to the right that leads to the tarmac lane up from **Gunnerside**. Go through this gate and you will see in the left-hand corner ahead a signpost by a small gated stile to **Low Row**. Go through the stile and into the next field, following the path through the next fields until you meet the last small wooden gate next to a larger metal one. Through this the land is much more open and immediately to the left you can see the houses of **Barf End**. Head straight on along the broad green track with great views opening up looking east down **Swaledale**.

5 Just before the next gate, turn onto a broad track going back down the hillside. Follow this all the way back to **Gunnerside**. At first the track is open as it crosses a large field before it passes a spring and then becomes a lane with drystone walls on either side. The way back is easy to follow now and on the way down passes the remains of some old cottages at **Lane Foot**. Keep on down until the track runs into the main road, turning right into **Gunnerside**.

20

Arkengarthdale & Fremington Edge

Heading down to Storthwaite Hall.

This walk takes you up onto the imposing Fremington Edge for great all-round views. It's quite a climb, but well worth the effort. In contrast, the return journey is down in the valley for some very pleasant walking along Arkle Beck. Reeth lies at the meeting place of Arkengarthdale and Swaledale. There are many walks around Reeth and up the Arkengarthdale valley so it's a popular venue for walkers. A picturesque market town with a history stretching back to Saxon times, its 18th-century houses, tea rooms and hotels clustered around the triangular village green make it one of the honey pots of the Dales. In May and June, Reeth hosts the Swaledale Festival, a two-week celebration of music and walks, and on the final Wednesday of August, the Reeth Show, an agricultural event, is held.

The remains of lead mines are to be seen all around Arkengarthdale. Lead has been mined here since at least Roman times, the last mine in the dale closing around 1912. Luckily most of the old industrial scars are overgrown so do not spoil the views or the walking.

Although a lot of sheep are in evidence around Reeth, there are still plenty of quiet tracks where your dog can safely stretch his legs off the lead. Apart

Dog factors

Distance: 9 miles.
Road walking: Short stretch from the hamlet of Booze into Langthwaite along a narrow quiet lane.
Livestock: Sheep are much in evidence around Reeth.
Stiles: Plenty of these but all are gated or there is an adjacent gate except one five-rung ladder stile (but there is an alternative route).
Nearest vets: Yoredale Vets, Leyburn.

from along Fremington Edge there are streams, springs and the large Arkle Beck in which to have a paddle.

Terrain

Steep ascent up Cuckoo Hill and some sections alongside Arkle Beck subject to flooding after heavy rain.

Where to park

There are lots of parking places in the middle of Reeth. **Sat nav:** DL11 6TN. **Maps:** OS Explorer OL30 Yorkshire Dales: North & East, Harvey Outdoor Yorkshire Dales: Dales North (GR SE038992).

How to get there

Travelling from the east up Swaledale, Reeth is on the main road (B6270) through the valley. You can also approach via Wensleydale over the Cliff Gate Road from Hawse. This is quite a challenging route in poor weather.

Nearest refreshments

The Black Bull, Reeth, welcomes dogs inside and has outside seating for sunny days. ☎ 01748 884213. See the website for the menu and opening times: www.theblackbullreeth.co.uk.

The Walk

1 Starting from the centre of **Reeth**, walk out of town (towards Fremington) until you cross over **Arkle Beck**. Look out for a footpath sign to **High Fremington** on your left that takes you diagonally across a large field and through the drystone wall opposite where it turns right to hug the wall and

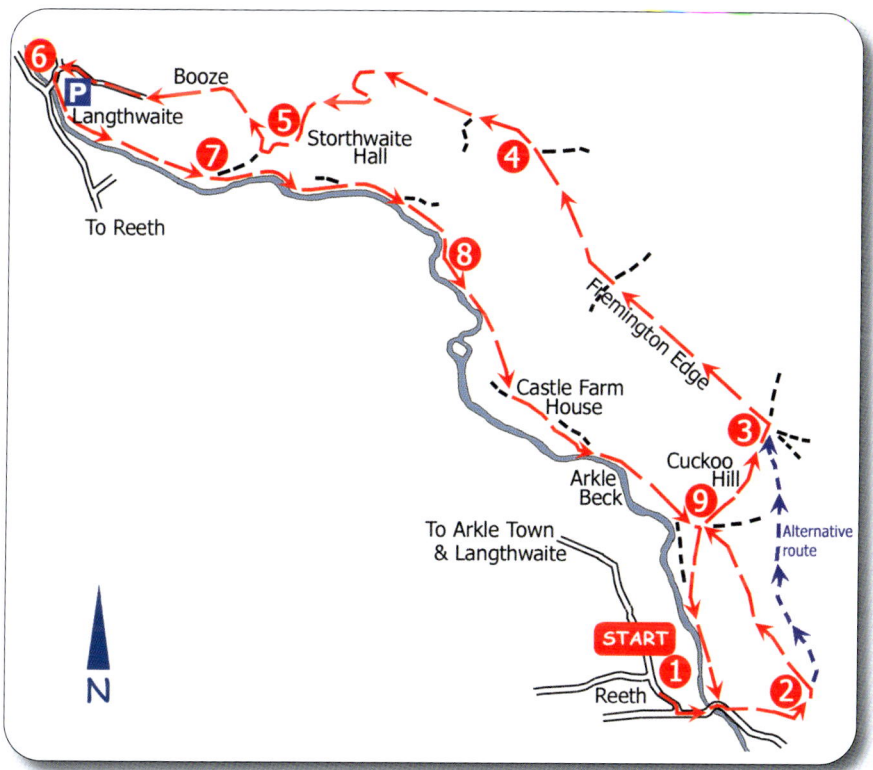

leads on through two more fields before emerging on a tarmac road. Turn left and then after 50 yards left again up another lane. Follow this uphill, turning left uphill again where it runs into another road. After 75 yards turn left into the track, signposted for **Arkengarthdale**.

2 If you wish to avoid a ladder stile continue up the tarmac road and follow it until it turns into a rough track that takes you past a disused quarry and eventually winds its way to **Fremington Edge** (3).

Assuming you are taking the more scenic route to the top, you can relax for a while and stroll along the track towards **Arkengarthdale** as it meanders along for about ½ mile. Stick to the main trackway until you meet a yellow-topped signpost showing public footpaths in three directions (point 9 – the left-hand direction takes you back to **Reeth** and is the path to follow on the way back). Looking right, directly up the hill is the way to go from here. Start off up this steep hill (**Cuckoo Hill**) and after about 50 yards a broken down drystone wall will come into view on your left. Walk up the hill parallel to this even when the path is indistinct and disappears from time to time. Eventually you run up to a more intact drystone wall that crosses your path and the only way over is via a five-rung ladder stile. It's the only one of its kind on the walk and hopefully your dog is not too muddy at this stage to be given a hand over it. The way ahead is steeper for a while but don't give up! Looking back, the views are getting bigger and better and it's a good reason to stop now and again and get your breath back.

Eventually you should see ahead a single signpost coming into view on the horizon. It's probably to your left as you continue to rise. Just before you get to it you will meet and join the track that continues up from the tarmac road you left at point 2. The signpost is showing you the way to **Fremington Edge** and **Hurst**, and the worst of the climbing is over as you walk towards a long drystone wall that runs along the entire edge. The track takes you up to a gate, go through this and turn left to follow the path alongside the wall.

3 Take time as you walk along the top to have a good look around as you can see for miles in all directions. Stay on the main path until the ground starts to descend gently again and eventually the broad path forks. Take the left fork up to the gate and go through it.

4 The heather now gives way to coarse grass on thin soil with lots of exposed rock. This area is scarred too by old lead mine workings. The path is marked with yellow-topped posts and starts to zig-zag as it descends through screes from old mine waste. As you descend towards **Storthwaite Hall** the village

Below Cuckoo Hill.

of **Booze** comes into view on the opposite side of the small valley formed by **Slei Gill**. As the path leads you up to a gate in the drystone wall, go through it in the direction of **Langthwaite** on the signpost. Continue in the same direction down the hill until the path leads into a lane.

5 At the bottom of the lane turn right to go round the farm buildings and then continue along the track through the farm gate and then across the footbridge over **Slei Gill** by the ford. Continue up the track for about 100 yards and turn right at the sign for **Slei Gill**. A short distance along this path turn left again at the next signpost to take the footpath up towards **Booze**. The path leads you through two drystone walls and up to a farm gate. Go through the gate and stay on this track, which later becomes a tarmac road, through **Booze** and all the way down to **Langthwaite**.

6 **Langthwaite** is an attractive little village with a pub (the **Red Lion Inn**) right in the centre that sadly does not allow dogs inside. There are a few benches outside though where you could relax a while if the weather is good. Take the lane opposite the **Red Lion** and then turn right down to the side of **Arkle Beck**. The track now follows the river and you need to stay with it past the sewage works and as it heads at first alongside, then up into the woods.

7 A short way into the wood, take the footpath to the right (marked by a post) and follow it downhill again. Later, where the track forks, take the left-hand path into a short tunnel under an embankment. On the other side continue across the field to another gate and ahead you will see a footbridge taking you over the lower end of **Slei Gill** that you crossed earlier. The path continues alongside the beck and runs up to woods where a signpost indicates that you should keep to the right alongside the river as you head back to **Reeth**. The next sections can be very wet and muddy after rain. Generally keep close to the beck and use the three flat wooden bridges to take you across the water and back, avoiding the really boggy areas.

8 Once back on the main path, keep heading down the valley, passing the sign post to Fremington, with the **Arkle Beck** running over broad gravel beds below as you climb gently up to **Castle Farm House** (over **Thorn Dale** on the OS map). Pass by the left side of the house and then turn left a few yards later to head across the fields towards the trees ahead. After going through a squeeze stile drop down past a ruined cottage with the trees now on your left. Follow the path until it joins the track that will lead you back to the bottom of **Cuckoo Hill**.

9 Turn right through the gate and follow the path across several fields to run against the **Arkle Beck**, back to the bridge on the B6270 where you started.

APPENDIX

Contact details for Small Animal Veterinary Practices in the Yorkshire Dales

Bainbridge Vets
Station Surgery, Askrigg, Leyburn, DL8 3BJ
☎ 01969 650263

Dalehead Veterinary Group
22 Station Road, Settle, North Yorkshire BD24 9AA
☎ 01729 823538

Dales Veterinary Centre
9 Courthouse St, Otley, West Yorkshire LS21 3AN
☎ 01943 463447

Holly House Veterinary Clinic
6 Regent Road, Ilkley, West Yorkshire LS29 9EA
☎ 01943 609285

Kingsway Veterinary Group
73 Otley Road, Skipton, North Yorkshire BD23 1HJ
☎ 01756 793224

Medivet Vet Hospital
Oak Beck Way, Harrogate HG1 3HU
☎ 01423 561414

Swale Veterinary Surgery
Unit 1, Fairfield Way, Gallowfields Trading Estate, Richmond DL10 4TB
☎ 01748 826600

Yoredale Vets
Unit 1-2, Leyburn Business Park, Harmby Road, Leyburn, DL8 5QA
☎ 01969 623024